WHISK ME AWAY

PROPER ROMANCE

WHISK ME AWAY

*A Cookbook of Romance
and Celebrations*

Michelle Wright

SHADOW
MOUNTAIN
PUBLISHING

As Julia Child once said,
"People who love to eat are
always the best people."
To all my friends and family
who have supported me and were
willing to taste test my recipes.

Image Credits:
Decorative elements: Vector Tradition/Adobe Stock, Little Monster 2070/Adobe Stock, afzal/Adobe Stock; viii: Hein Nouwens/Adobe Stock; 7, 55, 89, 115: Tartila/Adobe Stock; 11: Віталій Баріда/Adobe Stock; 15, 21, 43, 70, 77, 104, 123, 129, 130, 146, 157, 176, 182: lynea/Adobe Stock; 27: duncan1890/Getty Images; 101: Freepik/Adobe Stock, lynea/Adobe Stock; 142: mikroman6/Getty Images, Chelebi/Adobe Stock, Lisla/Adobe Stock, mutia/Adobe Stock; 169: max_776/Adobe Stock.

Photos: Shane Huntsman Photography
Stylist: Alexandra Bingham
Photography assistant: Easton Madsen
Production assistants: Laura Huff, Heidi Gordon, Heather Ward, Michelle Wright

Visit us at shadowmountain.com

PROPER ROMANCE is a registered trademark.

Library of Congress Cataloging-in-Publication Data
(CIP data on file)
ISBN 978-1-63993-378-5

Printed in China
RR Donnelley, Dongguan, China

10 9 8 7 6 5 4 3 2 1

CONTENTS

INTRODUCTION

ROMANTIC STORIES have a timeless appeal that has captivated readers for years. At their core, romance novels offer an escape from everyday life, transporting readers to different worlds, times, and places. This escapism provides a much-needed break from routine and stress, allowing readers to immerse themselves in a world where love and adventure await around every corner.

Beyond the allure of escape, romantic stories forge deep emotional connections. They can touch hearts on a personal level, resonating with a reader's own experiences, desires, and hopes. The characters' journeys through love, conflict, and resolution mirror the complexities of real-world relationships, offering insight and validation. This emotional depth allows readers to connect with the characters, experiencing their joys and heartbreaks as if they were their own.

Moreover, romantic stories celebrate the pleasure of a well-told love story. The joy derived from reading about love, passion, and connection should never be underestimated. Whether it's the thrill of a first kiss, the tension of unspoken feelings, or the satisfaction of a hard-won relationship, these moments captivate and delight.

Shadow Mountain Publishing decided to start publishing romance novels in 2012 with the first title under the Proper Romance brand: *Edenbrooke* by Julianne Donaldson. It became an instant bestseller;

fans couldn't get enough! Now, more than ten years later, and with more than sixty books by seventeen brilliantly talented authors, Proper Romance has become a must-have on every romance reader's shelf.

This cookbook is a celebration of that success, and it is designed to make hosting a romance-themed party fun and easy. Divided into five historical time periods, the recipes are further organized into specific parties—from a Regency tea party to a Victorian ball to a Steampunk-themed brunch to a Western BBQ buffet. Also included are recipes to celebrate Valentine's Day, a Spring weekend road trip, a summer Hawaiian luau, a fall feast, and a Christmas dinner and dessert extravaganza.

Also included are historical trivia and fun facts about food, traditions, and customs of the various time periods. Lists of notable novels for each era might start a book club conversation about the stories that sparked readers' imaginations through the years. Peruse the illustrations of the fashion trends of the day or invite party guests to join in the fun of one of the parlor games. Each recipe is also accompanied by a favorite quote from a Proper Romance novel.

Get ready to fall in love with these delicious dishes and celebrate with style, flair, and a banquet table full of romance.

HISTORY OF
WOMEN'S FASHION

1729   1730-40   1778-1779   1785

1790   1794   1797   1808   1814   1827

Georgian Era • 1714-1837
Regency Era • 1811-1820
Victorian Era • 1837-1901
Edwardian Era • 1901-1910

1829   1836   1840   1850   1854   1863   1869

1870   1873   1882   1892   1896   1905

REGENCY

THE REGENCY ERA, spanning from 1811 to 1820, was named after George IV, who served as the Prince Regent, and was a brief but dazzling era of elegance and refinement. Within this golden age, the aristocracy flourished amidst grand ballrooms and lush estates. It was a time when romantic entanglements blossomed against a backdrop of strict societal norms and unspoken passions. Dashing gentlemen courted ladies adorned in exquisite gowns. Love stories unfolded with a poignant blend of propriety and fervent emotion. These tales, often complicated by class distinctions and familial expectations, saw star-crossed lovers navigating the labyrinth of their hearts' desires, weaving narratives of enduring affection and timeless romance.

Tea Party

Classic Tea Sandwiches

CUCUMBER SANDWICHES

PREP TIME: 15 MIN · YIELDS 30 TEA SANDWICHES

1 loaf white bread, sliced	2 teaspoons fresh dill, chopped
3 tablespoons butter, softened	¼ teaspoon garlic powder
8 ounces cream cheese, softened	salt and pepper to taste
3 tablespoons mayonnaise	1 long English cucumber, thinly sliced
1 teaspoon fresh chives, chopped	

1. Trim crusts from bread slices. Spread a thin layer of butter on both sides of the slices.

2. With a mixer, mix cream cheese and mayonnaise in a bowl until smooth. Stir in chives, dill, and garlic powder. Salt and pepper to taste.

3. Spread the cream cheese mixture onto one side of buttered bread slices. Mixture should be similar in thickness to the bread.

4. Layer cucumbers on top of the cream cheese mixture.

5. Either top with another buttered bread slice or serve as an open-faced sandwich.

6. Cut sandwiches into small rectangles, about two-fingers thick, or from corner to corner for small triangles.

7. Serve immediately or cover and refrigerate up to 24 hours.

VARIATIONS

- Add sliced deli turkey, chicken, ham, or roast beef along with the cucumbers.
- Instead of chives and fresh dill, use a package of Italian seasoning mix.

NOTES

- The bread you use matters, and fresh is always best. While many varieties of tea sandwiches are made with white bread, you can use the bread you like best (pumpernickel, wheat, sourdough). The mixture also works with small dollar rolls.
- Filling can be prepared in advance. Store mixture in refrigerator and assemble sandwiches directly before serving.
- Sandwiches will stay fresh for a couple of hours if they are kept covered.

I poured the tea, the spicy ginger steam hitting my nose instantly. The underlying notes of jasmine flooded my head with visions of him.

ACROSS THE STAR-KISSED SEA
Arlem Hawks

EGG SALAD SANDWICHES

PREP TIME: 15 MIN · CHILL TIME: 1 HOUR · YIELDS 12 TEA SANDWICHES

4 eggs, hard boiled and peeled

4 tablespoons butter, softened, divided

1 tablespoon mayonnaise

1 pinch smoked paprika

6 slices potato bread

1. In a medium-size bowl, mash hard-boiled eggs.

2. In a separate bowl, mix 2 tablespoons butter, mayonnaise, and paprika.

3. Chill mixture for at least 1 hour.

4. When ready to serve, butter one side of each bread slice. Top with egg mixture and a second slice of buttered bread.

5. Remove crusts and cut sandwiches into rectangles or triangles.

CHICKEN SALAD SANDWICHES

PREP TIME: 15 MIN · CHILL TIME: 1 HOUR · YIELDS 12 TEA SANDWICHES

1 tablespoon mayonnaise

3 tablespoons olive oil

½ teaspoon thyme

2 teaspoons Dijon mustard

2 ounces grapes (green or purple), thinly sliced

2 (12.5-ounce) cans chicken breast, drained (or 3 cooked chicken breasts, shredded)

2 tablespoons butter, softened

6 slices white bread

8 ounces water chestnuts, sliced

1. In a large bowl, combine mayonnaise, olive oil, thyme, and Dijon mustard.

2. Add sliced grapes, shredded chicken, and mayonnaise mixture and mix well.

3. Chill mixture for at least 1 hour.

4. When ready to serve, butter one side of each bread slice. Add chicken mixture and a layer of water chestnuts. Top with a second slice of buttered bread.

5. Remove crusts and cut sandwiches into rectangles or triangles.

SALMON SANDWICHES

PREP TIME: 15 MIN · YIELDS 12 TEA SANDWICHES

1 tablespoon fresh dill (or 1 teaspoon dried dill)

1 pinch salt

2 ounces cream cheese, softened

2 tablespoons butter, softened

6 slices pumpernickel bread

½ English cucumber, thinly sliced

1 (4-ounce) package pre-sliced smoked salmon

1. In a medium-size bowl, mix dill and salt with softened cream cheese.

2. Butter one side of each bread slice. Add a layer of cucumbers.

3. Add a layer of thinly sliced salmon and top with a second slice of buttered bread.

4. Remove crusts and cut sandwiches into rectangles or triangles.

Regency Era Timeline

1811 George, Prince of Wales, becomes the Prince Regent
1812 War between the United Kingdom and the United States
1813 *Pride and Prejudice* by Jane Austen is published
1814 Gas lighting is introduced in London streets
1815 Napoleon is defeated at the Battle of Waterloo
1816 The fallout from the Mount Tambora eruption in
Indonesia creates the "year without a summer"
1818 Queen Charlotte dies
1819 Queen Victoria is born
1820 George III dies

NOTABLE NOVELS OF THE REGENCY ERA

Sense and Sensibility by Jane Austen (1811)
Pride and Prejudice by Jane Austen (1813)
Tales of the Dead by Sarah Elizabeth Utterson (1813)
Waverly by Sir Walter Scott (1814)
Mansfield Park by Jane Austen (1814)
The Wanderer: or, Female Difficulties by Fanny Burney (1814)
Emma by Jane Austen (1815)
Northanger Abbey by Jane Austen (1817)
Persuasion by Jane Austen (1817)
Frankenstein: or, The Modern Prometheus by Mary Shelley (1818)

Decadent Dips

SPINACH DIP

PREP TIME: 15 MIN · CHILL TIME: 1 HOUR · SERVES 8

1 (10-ounce package) frozen chopped spinach, thawed and drained

1 (6-ounce) can sliced water chestnuts, drained and chopped (optional)

2 cups sour cream

1 cup mayonnaise

1 (1-ounce) package ranch dressing mix

1 purple cabbage, hollowed out (optional)

1. Thaw frozen spinach and drain excess water.

2. Add chopped water chestnuts, if desired.

3. Combine all ingredients in a large mixing bowl. Chill for at least 1 hour.

4. If serving in a purple cabbage bowl, hollow out interior and cut off the bottom so it sits flat. Otherwise, serve in a bowl on a tray with tortilla chips, crackers, sliced vegetables, or toasted baguette slices.

SPINACH ARTICHOKE DIP

PREP AND COOKING TIME: 30 MIN · SERVES 8

8 ounces cream cheese, softened

¼ cup mayonnaise

¼ cup sour cream

1 teaspoon fresh minced garlic (or 1 clove)

⅔ cup finely grated Parmesan cheese

½ cup finely shredded mozzarella cheese

Pepper to taste

6 ounces frozen chopped spinach, thawed and drained

1 (14-ounce) can artichoke hearts, drained and chopped

1. In a large mixing bowl, combine cream cheese, mayonnaise, sour cream, garlic, Parmesan and mozzarella cheeses, and pepper. Stir in spinach and artichoke hearts.

2. Spray a 1-quart baking dish with nonstick cooking spray. Spread mixture evenly into prepared baking dish.

3. Bake at 350 degrees F. until heated through and cheese is melted, 20 to 25 minutes.

4. Serve with tortilla chips, crackers, sliced vegetables, or toasted baguette slices.

NOTE

· Dip can be made in advance and kept in the refrigerator. When ready to bake, let chilled mixture rest at room temperature 30 minutes, and then bake.

Peter lifted my hand between us, and, turning it over gently, he lifted it to his lips and pressed a kiss in the center of my palm. "I love you," he said, as tenderly as I'd ever heard his voice.

LAKESHIRE PARK
Megan Walker

8

CONTINUED ON PAGE 10

RED PEPPER HUMMUS

PREP AND CHILL TIME: 1 HOUR 15 MIN · SERVES 8

1 (15-ounce) can garbanzo beans, drained

4 ounces roasted red pepper

3 tablespoons lemon juice

1½ tablespoons tahini paste

1 clove garlic, minced

½ teaspoon cumin

½ teaspoon cayenne pepper

¼ teaspoon salt

1 tablespoon minced fresh parsley (optional)

5 to 6 olives minced (optional)

1 to 2 tablespoons chopped sun-dried tomatoes (optional)

1. In a food processor, puree garbanzo beans, red pepper, lemon juice, tahini paste, garlic, cumin, cayenne pepper, and salt until smooth.
2. Refrigerate at least 1 hour.
3. When ready to serve, garnish with fresh parsley, olives, and sun-dried tomatoes.
4. Serve with tortilla chips, crackers, sliced vegetables, or toasted baguette slices.

CREAM CHEESE FRUIT DIP

PREP: 5 MIN · CHILL TIME: 1 HOUR (OR OVERNIGHT)
YIELDS 16 (1 TABLESPOON) SERVINGS

8 ounces cream cheese, softened

1½ cups powdered sugar

¼ cup orange juice

Zest of 1 orange (optional)

1. With a mixer, beat cream cheese until smooth. Add powdered sugar, orange juice, and orange zest until well combined.
2. Cover and chill in refrigerator at least 1 hour.
3. Serve with your favorite seasonal fruit.

TOFFEE DIP

PREP TIME: 10 MIN · CHILL TIME: 1 HOUR (OR OVERNIGHT) · SERVES 12

8 ounces cream cheese, softened

¼ cup granulated sugar

¼ cup packed brown sugar

1 teaspoon vanilla extract

1 cup toffee bits (plain or chocolate)

1. With a mixer, beat cream cheese until smooth.
2. Add granulated sugar, brown sugar, and vanilla until smooth.
3. Fold in toffee bits. Chill at least 1 hour.
4. Serve with apple slices, purple or green grapes, or sliced strawberries.

Regency Game

FORFEIT
For 4+ players

Requires a deck of playing cards and a hat or container to hold the forfeits.

PREPARATION: Players sit in a circle with the deck of cards placed face down in the center alongside the forfeit container. Each player writes down at least 4 forfeits on individual slips of paper. (Forfeits are silly or embarrassing tasks, such as singing a song, telling a joke, or doing an impression.) Fold the forfeit papers and place in the container. The more forfeits in the container, the longer the game will last.

HOW TO PLAY: The first player draws a card from the deck and follows the instructions based on the cards suit:

- ♦ Diamonds: The player must give a compliment to someone in the group.

- ♣ Clubs: The player must perform a dare or challenge that is decided upon by the group.

- ♥ Hearts: The player must share a secret.

- ♠ Spades: The player must tell a joke or a funny story.

After drawing the card and following the instructions, the player must also draw a forfeit from the container and complete the task written on the slip of paper. Play continues clockwise around the circle, with each player drawing a card, following the instructions, and completing a forfeit.

The game ends when all the forfeits have been completed or the players have agreed on a predetermined number of rounds before starting.

Sweet Tart Lemon Bars

PREP AND COOKING TIME: 40 MIN · SERVES 24

CRUST

1 cup butter

½ cup powdered sugar

2 cups all-purpose flour

½ teaspoon salt

FILLING

4 large eggs, slightly beaten

2 cups granulated sugar

½ teaspoon baking powder

¼ cup flour

¼ cup fresh lemon juice (approximately 2 lemons)

Zest of 1 lemon

Powdered sugar

1. **For the crust:** In a large bowl, cream butter and powdered sugar. Add flour and salt.

2. Press crust firmly and evenly into a 9x13-inch pan.

3. Bake at 350 degrees F. for 15 to 20 minutes or until the edges are lightly browned.

4. **For the filling:** While crust is baking, combine eggs, sugar, baking powder, flour, lemon juice, and lemon zest.

5. Pour filling over crust and bake an additional 20 to 25 minutes.

6. Remove the bars from the oven; allow to cool completely.

7. When ready to serve, cut the lemon bars into squares and dust with powdered sugar.

VARIATION

- Instead of using lemon juice and zest, replace with key lime juice and lime zest.

When he smiled, the lines beside his eyes lengthened like the petals of a daisy. He wore his hair longer than was fashionable, and when it fell over his forehead, she wanted to brush it away.

Where on earth are these thoughts coming from? She was a vicar's daughter, for heaven's sake, nearly a spinster, and an inexperienced woman to boot.

MISS WILTON'S WALTZ
Josi S. Kilpack

NOTE

- You can halve the recipe for 12 bars in a 9-inch square pan. Bake the crust at 350 degrees F. for 15 minutes. Add the filling and bake an additional 18 to 20 minutes.

The Ultimate Guide to Herbal Teas

Herbal tea, also known as tisane, is a delightful and diverse category of beverages made from the infusion of various herbs, flowers, fruits, and spices steeped in hot water. Unlike traditional teas, which come from the Camellia sinensis plant, herbal teas can be caffeine-free and are often consumed for their unique flavors and medicinal properties. This guide will help you navigate the world of herbal tea, from its types and benefits to preparation tips and popular blends.

POPULAR TYPES OF HERBAL TEA

Herbal teas come in a wide variety, each with distinct flavors and health benefits:

- Made from the flowers of the **chamomile** plant, this tea is known for its calming and sleep-inducing properties.
- Made from **peppermint** leaves, this tea is refreshing and aids digestion.
- Also known as red bush tea, **rooibos** tea is native to South Africa and rich in antioxidants.
- Made from the dried petals of the **hibiscus** flower, this tea is known for its tart flavor and potential to lower blood pressure.
- Made from fresh or dried **ginger** root, this tea is renowned for its anti-inflammatory and digestive benefits.
- A member of the mint family, **lemon balm** tea has a mild lemon flavor and is often used to reduce stress and anxiety.
- Known for its soothing properties and floral aroma, **lavender** tea helps in relaxation and sleep.
- **Echinacea** is often used to boost the immune system and fight off colds.

HOW TO STEEP HERBAL TEA

Steeping herbal tea is simple, but here are some tips to ensure you get the best flavor and benefits:

- Use fresh, filtered water to avoid impurities.
- Generally, herbal teas should be prepared with water that has just reached a boil, around 200 to 212 degrees F. (93 to 100 degrees C.).
- Herbal teas typically need to steep longer than true teas, usually between 5 and 10 minutes, depending on the ingredients.
- Use 1 teaspoon of dried herbs or 1 tablespoon of fresh herbs per cup of water. Adjust to taste.

HERBAL TEA BLENDS

Here are some popular and easy-to-make herbal tea blends:

- Relaxation: chamomile, lavender, and lemon balm.
- Digestion: peppermint, ginger, and fennel.
- Immune boost: echinacea, elderberry, and ginger.
- Detox: dandelion root, burdock root, and nettle.
- Energy: ginseng, peppermint, and licorice root.

Creating your own herbal tea blends can be a fun and rewarding experience. Here are some tips:

- Combine herbs that complement each other. For example, chamomile pairs well with lavender, and peppermint goes well with ginger.
- Think about the health benefits you want to achieve and select herbs accordingly.
- Don't be afraid to try new combinations. Start with small batches to test your blends.

Picnic

Lemonades

SUNSHINE SWEET LEMONADE

PREP AND COOKING TIME: 20 MIN • CHILL TIME: 1 HOUR • SERVES 8

6 cups water, divided

1 cup granulated sugar

1 cup lemon juice

1 lemon, sliced (optional)

1. In a medium saucepan, heat 2 cups water and sugar over medium-high heat until sugar is dissolved. Stir often.
2. Place the simple syrup in a heat-resistant container and refrigerate at least 1 hour, until cold.
3. When ready to serve, add the simple syrup, lemon juice, and 4 cups water to a large pitcher. Stir to combine.
4. Serve over ice and garnish with sliced lemon.

FRUIT LEMONADE

PREP AND COOKING TIME: 35 MIN • CHILL TIME: 1 HOUR • SERVES 8

6 cups water, divided

1 cup granulated sugar

1 cup fresh fruit (strawberries, raspberries, blackberries, peaches)

1 cup lemon juice

1 lemon, sliced

1. In a medium saucepan, heat 2 cups water, sugar, and fruit over medium-high heat until sugar is dissolved. Stir often.
2. Bring mixture to a boil, reduce heat, and let simmer for 4 to 6 minutes until fruit is soft.
3. Remove pan from heat. Using a fork or potato masher, crush the fruit. Let mixture stand for 10 to 15 minutes to allow fruit to steep.
4. Strain the fruit syrup through a fine-mesh strainer into a medium-size bowl. Discard any pulp or seeds left in the strainer.
5. Place the fruit simple syrup in a heat-resistant container and refrigerate at least 1 hour, until cold.
6. When ready to serve, add the fruit simple syrup, lemon juice, and 4 cups of water to a large pitcher. Stir to combine.
7. Serve over ice and garnish with sliced lemon and additional fruit.

NOTES

• For a quicker lemonade, add 2 cups hot water and 1 cup of sugar to a large pitcher and stir until the sugar is dissolved. Add 1 cup lemon juice, 4 to 5 cups cold water, and 2 cups ice. Stir to combine. Serve.
• Bottled lemon juice can be used in a pinch, but it won't taste as fresh.

Heat soared through him, radiating from the point of contact to the ends of his fingers and toes. He was surprised he could not see it shooting out of him like rays of light. He wanted nothing more than to gather Miss Hawkins into his arms and seal their agreement with a kiss.

THE ART OF LOVE AND LIES
Rebecca Anderson

Hot Cross Buns

PREP AND COOKING TIME: 3 HOURS 30 MIN · YIELDS 1 DOZEN ROLLS

¾ cup warm water (110 degrees F.)

1 tablespoon active dry yeast

3 cups all-purpose flour

1 tablespoon instant powdered milk

¼ cup white sugar

1 large egg

1 large egg, separated and divided

¼ teaspoon salt

3 tablespoons butter, softened

¾ cup dried cranberries, diced small

1 teaspoon ground cinnamon

2 tablespoons water

½ cup confectioners' sugar

2 teaspoons milk

¼ teaspoon vanilla extract

1. Add warm water and yeast in the bowl of the mixer. Combine and then let sit between 5 and 7 minutes.

2. Add flour, milk powder, sugar, 1 whole egg, 1 egg white, and salt. Mix on low speed for 10 minutes, scraping down the dough occasionally.

3. Add butter, cranberries, and cinnamon. Mix for an additional 5 minutes.

4. Transfer dough to a greased bowl, cover with plastic wrap or a kitchen towel, and let sit for an hour or until dough is double in size.

5. Transfer dough to a floured surface. Punch down dough, re-cover with plastic wrap or a kitchen towel, and let rest for 10 minutes.

6. Shape double into 12 balls and place in a greased 9x12-inch pan. Re-cover with plastic wrap or a kitchen towel and let rise in a warm place until doubled, 35 to 40 minutes.

7. In a small bowl, mix 1 egg yolk with 2 tablespoons water; brush on dough balls.

8. Bake at 375 degrees F. until golden brown, about 20 minutes. Remove from pan immediately and cool on a wire rack.

9. Make glaze by mixing confectioners' sugar, milk, and vanilla until smooth. Place glaze in a piping bag or use a sandwich bag with the corner snipped off. Pipe a cross onto each roll.

She'd been fixing herself a cup of tea but stopped to stamp her foot stubbornly, a habit she'd only started once his father had passed. The new mannerism usually made him chuckle, but not today, for he felt entirely too vexed with the woman.

AN
INCONVENIENT
LETTER
Julie Wright

Tomato Cheddar Tart

PREP AND COOKING TIME: 1 HOUR · SERVES 4 TO 6

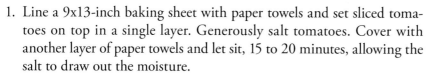

3 to 4 medium-to-large tomatoes, sliced very thinly

1 to 2 teaspoons salt

1 sheet puff pastry, thawed according to package instructions

⅓ cup prepared pesto

4 ounces (approximately 1 heaping cup) grated sharp cheddar cheese

fresh basil leaves (optional)

1. Line a 9x13-inch baking sheet with paper towels and set sliced tomatoes on top in a single layer. Generously salt tomatoes. Cover with another layer of paper towels and let sit, 15 to 20 minutes, allowing the salt to draw out the moisture.

2. Unfold the puff pastry onto a parchment-lined baking sheet or large cookie sheet. Prick the inside of the pastry with a fork every few inches, leaving a ½-inch border. Brush puff pastry with pesto, then cover with grated cheese. Remember to leave the outer border untouched.

3. Layer the tomatoes on top of the tart, allowing them to slightly overlap.

4. Bake at 400 degrees F. for 15 minutes, then rotate baking sheet in the oven and bake for another 10 to 15 minutes until puff pastry is browned and puffed.

5. Allow tart to cool for 10 to 15 minutes before cutting into slices. If desired, garnish with fresh basil leaves.

6. Serve immediately or at room temperature.

He rose up, and she prepared herself to be thoroughly kissed. But he stopped a fraction of an inch from her mouth, leaving her hungry. "I love you, Bianca," he said in a hoarse whisper that warmed her like the sun. "And I look forward to a lifetime of adventure with you by my side."

A LADY'S FAVOR
Josi S. Kilpack

> **DID YOU KNOW?** The most popular chef of the Regency era was Marie-Antoine Carême, who cooked for both Napoleon and the Prince Regent.

He looked intently into my eyes, as though he would write the words on my heart if he could. "You are bright and fun and delightfully unexpected. You are brave and compassionate and selfless. And you are lovely beyond measure. I want you, all of you, just the way you are." He drew in a breath. "If you will have me."

Something happened to me in that moment. Doubt was banished and hope became certainty. It overwhelmed me, and I found myself laughing and crying at once.

I was clearly unraveled, but Philip did not seem to mind at all. He wiped my tears, and he kissed me again, and again, and whispered things too sublime to repeat, until I was thoroughly convinced he was madly in love with me, Marianne Daventry, a girl with no great figure, too many freckles, and a propensity for twirling. And then I knew I had met my match.

EDENBROOKE
Julianne Donaldson

Mini No-Bake Cheesecakes

PREP AND COOKING TIME: 30 MIN · CHILL TIME: 3 HOURS
YIELDS 24 MINI CHEESECAKES

GRAHAM CRACKER CRUST

2 cups graham cracker crumbs

⅓ cup brown sugar

½ cup butter, melted

FILLING

1 cup heavy whipping cream

16 ounces cream cheese, softened

⅓ cup granulated sugar

2 tablespoons sour cream

½ teaspoon vanilla extract

1 teaspoon lemon juice

1. Line 2 standard-size muffin tins with cupcake liners.

2. **For the crust:** Pour graham cracker crumbs in a medium bowl and whisk in brown sugar and melted butter until combined. Spoon 1½ tablespoons of the crust mixture into each cupcake liner and use the back of a spoon to pack it down tightly.

3. Bake the crusts at 350 degrees F. for 5 minutes. (If desired, let the crusts cool for 10 minutes before adding the filling.)

4. **For the filling:** Using a stand mixer or hand mixer, whip the heavy cream on medium-high speed, or until stiff peaks are reached, about 3 to 5 minutes. Set aside. In a separate bowl, use a stand mixer or hand mixer to beat the cream cheese until smooth. Scrape down the sides and bottom of the bowl. Add sugar. Beat on medium speed until smooth and creamy. Add the sour cream, vanilla extract, and lemon juice. Mix for 1 minute.

5. Slowly fold the whipped cream into the cheesecake filling until combined. (Don't deflate the air out of the whipped cream.)

6. Using a cookie scoop or spoon, place 2 tablespoons of the filling into the crumb-lined muffin tins. Smooth to make flat.

7. Refrigerate cheesecakes in the pans for at least 3 hours.

8. When ready to serve, top with whipped cream, fresh fruit, pie filling, caramel or chocolate sauce, or a citrus curd.

NOTE
· Cheesecakes can be stored in an airtight container in the refrigerator for up to 3 days.

VARIATIONS
· Use a vanilla wafer cookie or a chocolate sandwich cookie in place of the graham cracker crust.
· In step 4, add ½ cup mini chocolate chips, ⅓ cup fruit jam, or ⅓ cup lemon, lime, or orange curd.
· Can be served in a larger dessert dish.

He had a crop of ink-black hair, wild curls looking as if he had just run his hands through them, and a sharp jaw with the dark stubble of a man who had yet to shave.

Thick brows perched above those blue eyes, balanced with a strong nose. He might have been handsome if not for that irritating, lopsided grin.

And he was absolutely *not* what I had pictured a thief-taker would look like.

A HEART WORTH STEALING
Joanna Barker

At the Ball

Lemon Bundt Cake

PREP AND COOKING TIME: 1 HOUR 10 MIN · SERVES 6 TO 8

CAKE

2 cups all-purpose flour

1 (3.4-ounce) box instant lemon
  pudding dry mix

1½ teaspoon baking powder

1 teaspoon Kosher salt

1½ cups granulated sugar

3 large eggs, room temperature

½ cup vegetable oil, or lemon-
  infused olive oil

1 cup sour cream, room temperature

1 teaspoon vanilla extract

zest of 1 lemon

2 tablespoons lemon juice

GLAZE

1 cup powdered sugar

3 tablespoons whole milk

1 tablespoon lemon juice

1 tablespoon lemon zest

1 tablespoon vanilla extract

1. **For the cake:** In a large bowl, combine flour, dry lemon pudding mix, baking powder, and salt. Whisk together. Set aside.

2. In a medium bowl, whisk together sugar and eggs until well blended. Add oil, sour cream, vanilla, lemon zest, and lemon juice. Whisk until combined.

3. Fold the wet ingredients into the dry ingredients. Don't overmix; there will be lumps.

4. Pour cake batter into a 10-inch Bundt pan sprayed with nonstick cooking spray. Use a spoon to smooth the batter, or gently tap the pan against the counter to evenly distribute the batter.

5. Bake at 325 degrees F. for 1 hour, or until a toothpick inserted comes out clean. Allow to cool in the pan for 10 minutes then carefully invert the pan onto a wire rack. Allow cake to cool completely before glazing.

6. **For the glaze:** In a medium bowl, combine powdered sugar, milk, lemon juice, lemon zest, and vanilla. Whisk until well combined and smooth.

7. Place the cake on a platter or cake stand. Pour lemon glaze over cooled cake. Serve.

She touched her fingertips to her lips and remembered the kiss and the breathlessness that had ensued. She had nearly sunk to the ground when he'd left her outside, her knees weak and her heart pounding.

MY FAIR GENTLEMAN
Nancy Campbell Allen

DID YOU KNOW? Candles were sold in either four-hour or six-hour burn lengths, which often determined how long a ball would last.

REGENCY: At the Ball

Fashion of the Day

1811 to 1820

Cravat

Vest

Overcoat

Breeches

Walking stick

Riding boots

Top hat

Curls

Short sleeve

Empire waist

Gloves

Poke bonnet

Floor-length skirt

Embellishments

Butter Cake with Almond Glaze

PREP AND COOKING TIME: 1 HOUR 35 MIN · SERVES 12

CAKE

2 cups granulated sugar

1 cup butter, softened to room temperature

4 eggs

1 tablespoon vanilla

3 cups all-purpose flour

1 teaspoon salt

1 teaspoon baking powder

½ teaspoon baking soda

1 cup buttermilk

GLAZE

2 teaspoons almond extract

2 tablespoons water

¾ cup granulated sugar

⅓ cup butter

1. **For the cake:** Place all cake ingredients in the bowl of a stand mixer. Mix on low for 30 seconds and then increase to medium speed and mix for 3 minutes.

2. Spray a 10-inch Bundt pan with nonstick cooking spray and flour very generously.

3. Pour batter into prepared pan and bake at 325 degrees F. for 65 to 75 minutes or until a cake tester or toothpick inserted in the center comes out clean.

4. Allow cake to cool in cake pan for 10 minutes.

5. **For the glaze:** Combine all glaze ingredients into a small saucepan over medium-low heat. Stir continuously until butter is melted and sugar is dissolved. Do not boil.

6. Using a skewer or knife, poke holes all over the warm cake and cover evenly with the glaze.

VARIATIONS

• Vanilla extract or coconut extract can be used in place of almond extract.
• Serve cake with whipping cream and fresh peaches.
• Instead of plain whipping cream, fold 1 cup lemon curd into whipping cream and serve with assorted berries.
• Add mini chocolate chips to the cake in step 1 and top with chocolate sauce instead of the glaze.

She held his gaze a moment too long, and a kind of sweet tension settled in the air around them. She might speak of Mr. Bentley, but her gaze said something else entirely. Her lips tugged at the corners, drawing his eyes to them. Miles wanted nothing more than to lean over and kiss her.

THE GENTLEMAN'S CONFESSION
Anneka R. Walker

Coconut Macaroons

PREP AND COOKING TIME: 35 MIN
YIELDS APPROXIMATELY 30 COOKIES

10 ounces sweetened shredded coconut

¾ cup sweetened condensed milk

1 teaspoon vanilla extract

¼ teaspoon coconut or almond extract

¼ teaspoon salt

2 large egg whites, room temperature

4 ounces semisweet chocolate (optional)

1. In a large mixing bowl, add shredded coconut, sweetened condensed milk, vanilla, coconut extract, and salt. Stir until well-combined.

2. In a separate dry, grease-free bowl, beat egg whites with a mixer starting on low speed, gradually increasing to high speed until stiff peaks are formed.

3. Using a spatula, gently fold egg whites into coconut mixture until combined.

4. Line 2 large cookie sheets with parchment paper. Drop mixture by small cookie scoop, about 1 inch apart.

5. Bake at 325 degrees F. for 20 to 25 minutes or until edges just begin to turn light golden-brown.

6. Allow cookies to cool completely on cookie sheet.

7. If using chocolate, melt chocolate in a microwave-safe bowl in 20-second intervals (stirring in between) until chocolate is melted and smooth. Drizzle chocolate over cooled macaroons or dip the bottoms of the cookies in chocolate. Transfer to a baking sheet lined with parchment paper and allow chocolate to solidify before serving.

He pulled her close, deliciously so, and she adjusted her arm as he took her hand. They danced in perfect time with the music flowing through the ballroom doors, over the veranda, and down the stone stairs.

A HEART REVEALED
Josi S. Kilpack

NOTES
- ¾ cup of sweetened condensed milk is not a whole can.
- For a finer texter of the macaroons, process coconut in a food processor until finely shredded—about 15 1-second pulses.
- Macaroons can be stored in an airtight container at room temperature for up to 1 week. They may also be tightly wrapped and frozen for up to 3 months.

Enchanting Éclair Cake

PREP AND COOKING TIME: 1 HOUR 30 MIN
CHILL TIME: 9 HOURS (OR OVERNIGHT) · SERVES 12

CRUST

½ cup butter

1 cup water

1 cup all-purpose flour

4 large eggs

FILLING

8 ounces cream cheese, softened

3 cups milk

1 (5.1-ounce) box instant vanilla pudding

TOPPING

1 cup cold heavy whipping cream or heavy cream

2 tablespoons powdered sugar

½ teaspoon vanilla extract

Pinch of salt

Chocolate sauce

1. **For the crust:** In a medium saucepan, melt butter in water over medium heat. Bring to a boil. Remove pan from heat and stir in flour. Mix in one egg at a time, mixing completely before adding each egg.

2. Lightly grease a 9x13-inch glass baking pan with nonstick cooking spray. Spread mixture into prepared pan, covering the bottom and sides evenly. The mixture will be very wet.

3. Bake crust at 400 degrees F. for 25 to 35 minutes or until golden brown.

4. Remove from oven and let cool. It is normal to have bubbles in the crust.

5. **For the filling:** Whip cream cheese in a medium bowl until smooth. In a separate bowl, blend milk and pudding with an electric mixer for 3 minutes. Chill at least 8 hours or overnight until set.

6. Once pudding is set, slowly mix pudding into cream cheese. Blend until smooth.

7. Cool in fridge for at least 1 hour.

8. When crust is completely cooled, add in filling, covering the bottom of the crust.

9. **For the topping:** Using a hand mixer, whip heavy cream, powdered sugar, vanilla extract, and salt on medium speed until medium peaks form, about 3 to 4 minutes.

10. Top cake with whipping cream and drizzle with chocolate sauce.

Moonlight cast shadows on his face, highlighting his cheekbones and straight nose. Even in dim light, and wearing clothes not befitting his station, he was extraordinarily handsome.

I could not resist him.

SUMMERHAVEN
Collector's Edition
Tiffany Odekirk

VARIATIONS

- Black Forest Éclair Cake: Use chocolate pudding and a cherry or raspberry pie filling, or use coconut pudding with chocolate sauce and top with shredded coconut.
- Top cake with a sprinkling of mini chocolate chips.
- Change up the flavors by using a cheesecake, lemon, or French vanilla pudding.

NOTE

- This cake can be made in a muffin tin for individual servings. Bake at 400 degrees F. for 15 to 20 minutes.

DID YOU KNOW? When the waltz became popular during the Regency era, it was considered scandalous because it represented a significant departure from the more formal and structured dances that preceded it where the dancers had little contact with each other. The waltz, on the other hand, allowed the dancers to hold each other close.

Dinner Party

Green Bean Almondine with Rice Pilaf

PREP AND COOKING TIME: 1 HOUR 15 MIN · SERVES 6

GREEN BEANS

½ pound fresh green beans or 1 (9-ounce) package frozen cut or French-style green beans

2 tablespoons slivered or sliced almonds

1 tablespoon butter

1 teaspoon lemon juice

RICE PILAF

2 tablespoons butter

1 cup uncooked rice

⅓ cup finely chopped celery

¼ cup finely chopped onion

3 cups chicken broth

2 tablespoons chopped parsley

¼ cup slivered or sliced almonds

1. **For the green beans:** If using fresh green beans, prepare the beans by cutting off both ends. Wash.

2. In a medium-size saucepan, cook beans, covered in a small amount of boiling water, 10 to 12 minutes, or until crisp and tender. Drain. (If using frozen green beans, cook according to package instructions.)

3. While beans are cooking, in a small saucepan, cook almonds in butter, stirring frequently. Heat on medium-high until almonds are toasted golden brown.

4. Remove almonds from heat. Stir in lemon juice.

5. Mix almonds with green beans and serve.

6. **For the rice pilaf:** In a large frying pan, melt butter over high heat.

7. Add rice, celery, and onion. Stir and cook for 10 to 15 minutes or until mixture is slightly softened.

8. Add chicken broth. Cover and simmer on low heat for 15 to 18 minutes or until moisture has been absorbed and rice is tender.

9. Gently stir in parsley and almonds and serve.

NOTE
· If using fresh lemon juice, add a dash of lemon zest to the almonds.

He was handsome—golden-haired, blue-eyed, tall and lean—and he carried himself with the arrogant confidence of youth and freedom. There was a roughness to him too, however, a sense that he didn't quite belong. It made her wonder where he'd come from.

RAKES AND ROSES
Josi S. Kilpack

Lemon Roasted Chicken

PREP AND COOKING TIME: 2 HOURS 45 MIN · SERVES 4 TO 6

4- to 5-pound whole chicken

1 lemon

½ cup salted butter, melted

¼ cup lemon juice

2 tablespoons honey

2 teaspoons dried rosemary

1 clove garlic, minced

1. Rinse chicken and pat dry. Make sure the cavity is clear of any packing materials. Place chicken breast-side up in a roasting pan.

2. Slice lemon into quarters and place in the chicken's chest cavity.

3. In a small bowl, combine melted butter, lemon juice, honey, rosemary, and garlic. Brush half of butter mixture on chicken.

4. Roast uncovered at 375 degrees F. for 1 hour.

5. Remove from oven and brush chicken with the remaining butter mixture. Loosely cover the chicken with foil and bake for an additional hour, until interior temperature reaches 165 degrees F.

6. Remove from oven and discard lemons from inside the cavity.

7. Let the chicken rest for 10 minutes before serving.

He had changed for dinner and looked more handsome than I had ever seen him. He was soon by my side, smelling of that expensive cologne. He took my hand in his. "You look lovely."

PROMISED
Leah Garriott

NOTES
· If you don't have a roasting pan, a 9x13-inch baking pan will work.
· Once the chicken is fully cooled, you can shred the meat and store it in an airtight container in the refrigerator for up to 2 days.

Know Your Table

A Bread Plate and Knife

B Salad Fork

C Dinner Fork

D Dessert Fork

E Dinner Plate

F Salad Plate

G Saucer

H Napkin

I Knife

J Teaspoon

K Soup Spoon

L Water Goblet

M Punch Glass

N Mocktail Glass

Honey Glazed Ham

PREP AND COOKING TIME: 3 HOURS 10 MIN · SERVES 8

½ cup butter

1 cup brown sugar

¼ cup honey or maple syrup

¼ cup pineapple juice

½ teaspoon cinnamon

8 pounds bone-in spiral-cut ham

1. In a small saucepan, add butter, brown sugar, honey, pineapple juice, and cinnamon. Bring to a simmer over medium heat and cook for 5 to 7 minutes, or until glaze is syrupy.

2. Place ham in a roasting pan coated with cooking spray and cover with half the glaze. Reserve the remaining glaze for later use.

3. Cover ham with aluminum foil and bake at 325 degrees F. for 2½ hours.

4. Uncover ham and cover with remaining glaze. (If the reserved glaze has started to harden, soften in microwave for 15 to 30 seconds.)

5. Increase oven to 400 degrees F. and return uncovered ham to the oven. Bake an additional 15 to 20 minutes or until glaze is caramelized and browned.

6. Transfer ham to a serving platter. Spoon pan drippings over the ham. Slice and serve.

VARIATIONS

• Instead of pineapple juice, use cranberry or orange juice.

I'd been kissed before. I'd seen the look in a man's eyes, felt the tempting lure of anticipation that strung between a couple. And I was quite certain that Nathaniel Denning wanted to kiss me.

SO TRUE A LOVE
Joanna Barker

Hearty Beef Stew

PREP AND COOKING TIME: 6½ HOURS TO 8½ HOURS · SERVES 4 TO 6

1 (1.5-ounce) package dried onion soup

1 (12-ounce) can cream of mushroom soup

1 (12-ounce) can cream of celery soup

1 (8-ounce) can tomato sauce

2 pounds stew meat or roast, cut into bite-size pieces

8 medium potatoes, peeled and cut into bite-size pieces

8 large carrots, peeled and cut into bite-size pieces

2 bay leaves

1. In a large bowl, mix soups and tomato sauce together into a sauce.

2. In a large slow cooker, add stew meat, potatoes, and carrots.

3. Add the soup sauce and bay leaves.

4. Cook on low for 6 to 8 hours.

"I swear to you, Miss Blake, if you can't find a means of graciously accepting what I am generously offering you, I'll dump that bowl of stew right over your head. And what's more, I will enjoy it."

ASHES ON THE MOOR
Sarah M. Eden

NOTES
· If the stew meat is frozen, set slow cooker to high and cook for 8 hours.
· You can substitute other soups depending on the flavor you want. For a spicier flavor, substitute the cream of mushroom soup for a cheddar cheese soup.
· For a saucier stew, add one more can of soup. You may need to add salt before serving.

Mind Your
Table Manners

IN REGENCY ENGLAND, table manners reflected one's social standing and upbringing, providing a window into the era's intricate social hierarchies and genteel customs. Dining was a ceremonious affair, where every action, from the placement of utensils to the passing of dishes, adhered to a strict etiquette. Mastery of these table manners was seen as a mark of refinement and sophistication, essential for navigating the social intricacies of Regency society.

1. Do not be late: Arriving on time for dinner was essential. Being late was seen as disrespectful to the host and other guests.

2. Where you sit matters: Guests were seated according to their social status and relationships. The host and hostess typically sat at opposite ends of the table, with the most important guests seated closest to them on their right.

3. Straighten your shoulders: Sitting upright without leaning on the table or slouching was expected. Good posture was a sign of good breeding.

4. Napkins are important: Napkins were placed on laps at the beginning of the meal and used discreetly to dab the mouth. They were never tucked into the collar or used to wipe the face. Prior to the

meal, ladies would take off their gloves and place them under the napkins on their lap.

5. Please pass the food: Food was passed to the right. It was important to serve oneself moderately to ensure there was enough for everyone.

6. A guide to cutlery: Forks were held in the left hand and knives in the right. Forks were used to bring food to the mouth, not knives.

7. Keep the conversation light: Polite, light conversation was encouraged, particularly topics that could be enjoyed by all guests. Controversial or personal topics were avoided.

8. No elbows on the table: Resting elbows on the table was considered rude. Hands were expected to be kept in the lap when not in use.

9. The host is always in charge: Guests waited for the host or hostess to start eating before they would begin. Similarly, they waited for the host to finish before getting up from the table.

10. Food should not be seen *or* heard: Eating quietly without making noise was important. Slurping, chewing loudly, or talking with a full mouth was considered bad manners.

Raspberry Balsamic Ice Cream

PREP AND COOKING TIME: 1 HOUR
CHILL TIME: 4 HOURS (OR OVERNIGHT) · YIELDS 12 ½-CUP SERVINGS

2 cups heavy cream

4 large egg yolks

½ cup granulated sugar

⅛ teaspoon salt

1 teaspoon vanilla extract

2 cups raspberries, washed

¼ cup brown sugar

3 tablespoons raspberry balsamic vinegar

1. In a medium saucepan, simmer cream on medium-low heat for 6 to 8 minutes until it reaches 165 degrees F. Remove pan from heat.

2. In a mixing bowl, whisk egg yolks, granulated sugar, salt, and vanilla. Whisking constantly, slowly pour the hot cream into the yolk mixture. Return to pan and gently cook on medium-low heat until mixture is thick enough to coat the back of a spoon (about 165 degrees F.).

3. In a blender, puree raspberries, brown sugar, and balsamic vinegar. Puree should be on the sweet side, with some underlying tartness. If necessary, add either more sugar or more balsamic vinegar to taste.

4. Pour puree into a separate saucepan and cook on medium-low heat until fruit mixture thickens, about 10 minutes. Remove from heat.

5. Allow both mixtures to cool to room temperature.

6. Combine cream base and fruit puree. Cover and chill at least 4 hours or overnight.

7. Churn mixture in an ice cream machine and freeze according to manufacturer's instructions.

8. Frozen ice cream can be served immediately, or it can be made ahead of time and stored in freezer until ready to serve.

VARIATIONS

- Instead of raspberry, use strawberries with a strawberry balsamic or peaches with a peach balsamic.

He stepped even closer, and now I could see the faint stubble along his jaw line, and I had to admit that he was handsome. He was very handsome, in fact.

BLACKMOORE
Julianne Donaldson

DID YOU KNOW? One of the most popular flavors of ice cream during the Regency era was Parmesan cheese.

VICTORIAN

THE VICTORIAN ERA, spanning from 1837 to 1901, was a time of profound romance and elegance. Amidst the grandeur of Queen Victoria's reign, people were guided by intricate social rituals and enjoyed opulent balls where love blossomed under the soft glow of gaslights. Gentlemen, with their impeccable manners and tailored suits, pursued the affections of graceful ladies in lavish gowns adorned with lace and silk. Against a backdrop of blossoming gardens and stately manors, love stories flourished, often tinged with the excitement of forbidden passions and whispered secrets. The era's strict societal norms only heightened the thrill of romance, as hearts sought connection in a world of refinement and beauty, creating timeless tales of enduring love.

High Tea

The Perfect Tea Cookie

PREP AND COOKING TIME: 30 MIN · CHILL TIME: 1 HOUR
YIELDS ABOUT 4 DOZEN COOKIES

1 cup butter, softened

2 cups powdered sugar, divided

2 cups all-purpose flour, divided

2 teaspoons vanilla extract

⅛ teaspoon salt

1 cup pecans or walnuts, finely chopped

1. In a stand mixer or large mixing bowl, beat butter and ½ cup powdered sugar at medium speed until light and fluffy. Gradually add 1 cup flour, vanilla, and salt. Beat at low speed until well blended. Stir in remaining flour and chopped nuts.

2. Wrap dough in plastic wrap and refrigerate 1 hour, or until firm.

3. With a small cookie scoop, place dough on a large cookie sheet lined with parchment paper.

4. Bake at 350 degrees F. for 12 to 15 minutes, or until pale golden-brown. Let cookies stand on cookie sheet for 2 minutes.

5. Place 1 cup powdered sugar in a 9x13-inch dish. Transfer hot cookies to dish and roll in powdered sugar, coating well. Let cookies cool in powdered sugar.

6. When ready to serve, sift additional powdered sugar on cookies if needed.

VARIATIONS

- Use 1 cup mini chocolate chips, toffee bits, or crème de menthe baking chips instead of nuts.
- Use pistachios or almonds instead of pecans or walnuts.
- For a citrus-flavored cookie, replace vanilla extract with 1 teaspoon lemon juice, ¼ teaspoon lemon extract, and 2 teaspoons lemon zest.

DID YOU KNOW? While the first gothic novel was published in 1764, the genre found great popularity in 1847 with the publication of *Jane Eyre* by Charlotte Brontë.

NOTE

- Store cookies in an airtight container. Cookies will also freeze for up to one month.

Evangeline leaned against him. "I still find myself amazed at my good fortune. To have found the both of you here. That Ronan allowed me into his life. That you decided to love me in the end, no matter our difficult beginning."

ASHES ON THE MOOR,
Collector's Edition
Sarah M. Eden

VICTORIAN: High Tea

51

Scrumptious Scones

PREP AND COOKING TIME: 1 HOUR · CHILL TIME: 15 TO 20 MIN
YIELDS 8 TO 16 SCONES

SCONES

½ cup granulated sugar

2½ teaspoons baking powder

½ teaspoon salt

2 cups all-purpose flour

½ cup butter, frozen

½ cup heavy cream

1 large egg

1 teaspoon vanilla extract

1½ cups fruit, diced (cranberries, rhubarb, berries, apricots, or peaches)

2 to 3 tablespoons turbinado sugar

GLAZE

½ teaspoon vanilla extract

2 to 3 tablespoons heavy cream or milk

1 cup powdered sugar

Pinch of salt

almond extract (optional)

lemon extract (optional)

coconut extract (optional)

1. **For the scones:** Whisk sugar, baking powder, salt, and flour together in a large mixing bowl.

2. Using a grater, shred frozen butter onto a plate. Add butter to flour mixture and combine with your fingers, a fork, or pastry cutter until the mixture comes together in small crumbs. Place in the refrigerator.

3. In a small bowl or measuring cup, whisk heavy cream, egg, and vanilla extract. Add to the flour mixture. Add fruit and mix until combined.

4. To make drop scones: Drop balls of dough (about ¼ cup each) approximately 3 inches apart on a large cookie sheet lined with parchment paper.

5. To make wedges: On a lightly floured surface, shape dough into a ball with floured hands. If dough is too sticky, add a little more flour. If too dry, add 1 to 2 tablespoons of heavy cream. Flatten ball into an 8-inch disc and cut into 8 wedges.

6. Brush scones with heavy cream and sprinkle turbinado sugar on top.

7. Place scones on cookie sheet and refrigerate 15 to 20 minutes.

8. After scones have chilled, bake at 400 degrees F. for 20 to 25 minutes, or until golden brown around the edges and lightly brown on top.

9. Remove from oven and cool for 5 minutes on a wire rack.

CONTINUED ON PAGE 54

She felt herself sway toward him, just the tiniest of fractions closer, as though he were a magnet pulling her in. His eyes searched hers, traveled over her face, her hair, and she wished he would take his hands from his pockets and touch her cheek.

TO CAPTURE HIS HEART
Nancy Campbell Allen

VICTORIAN: High Tea

10. **For the glaze:** Whisk the vanilla extract, heavy cream, powdered sugar, and salt together. If mixture is too thick, add another tablespoon of heavy cream. Drizzle immediately over scones.

NOTES
- Scones can be made the night before. Once scones are made, refrigerate in an airtight container.
- Step 6 is optional if using a glaze for the scones.

VARIATIONS
- Fruit can be fresh or frozen; however, do not thaw frozen fruit. If using apples or peaches, make sure to peel and chop fruit before adding it to the dough.
- In step 3, add cinnamon and a pinch of nutmeg, or chocolate chips or cinnamon chips.

DID YOU KNOW? Penny dreadfuls brought stories of mystery, murder, romance, and the supernatural to the working-class people of Victorian London and included characters such as Sweeney Todd and the urban legend of Spring-Heeled Jack.

Victorian Era Timeline

1837 Queen Victoria ascends to the throne

1838 The practice of slavery is abolished in the British Empire

1840 Queen Victoria marries Prince Albert

1840 The "penny post" implemented

1845 Irish potato famine begins

1851 The Great Exhibition opens in London

1853 Crimean War begins

1863 London Underground opens

1869 The Suez Canal opens

1876 Alexander Graham Bell patents the telephone

1880 The Elementary Education Act makes school attendance mandatory for children

1888 Jack the Ripper terrorizes Whitechapel

1901 Queen Victoria dies

NOTABLE NOVELS OF THE VICTORIAN ERA

Jane Eyre by Charlotte Brontë (1847)

Wuthering Heights by Emily Brontë (1847)

A Christmas Carol by Charles Dickens (1843)

David Copperfield by Charles Dickens (1850)

North and South by Elizabeth Gaskell (1855)

The Woman in White by Wilkie Collins (1859)

Great Expectations by Charles Dickens (1861)

Alice's Adventures in Wonderland by Lewis Carroll (1865)

Middlemarch by George Eliot (1871)

A Study in Scarlet by Arthur Conan Doyle (1887)

The Picture of Dorian Gray by Oscar Wilde (1890)

Dracula by Bram Stoker (1897)

Spiced Pear Cheesecake

PREP AND COOKING TIME: 1½ TO 2 HOURS · CHILL TIME: OVERNIGHT
SERVES 8

2 cups crushed gingersnaps

6 tablespoons unsalted butter, room temperature

4 small pears, peeled, cored, and thinly sliced

¼ teaspoon ground cinnamon

⅛ teaspoon ground nutmeg

16 ounces cream cheese, room temperature

1¼ cups sugar, divided

2 large eggs, room temperature

3 teaspoons vanilla extract, divided

1 cup sour cream, room temperature

Whipped cream

As she turned the lovely pear over in her fingers, she remembered Alexander's glance at her over dinner that night earlier in the week, the feeling that they'd shared a moment of intimacy.

ISABELLE AND ALEXANDER
Rebecca Anderson

1. In a bowl, mix crushed gingersnaps with butter. Press mixture into a 9-inch baking pan, covering the bottom and sides. Bake at 350 degrees F. for 10 minutes. Cool completely.

2. Increase oven temperature to 400 degrees F. In a small bowl, toss together pears, cinnamon, and nutmeg. Place in an oven-safe dish and roast 30 minutes until the pears are soft and caramelized. Remove from oven and cool completely.

3. Layer caramelized pear slices on top of the crust.

4. Reduce oven temperature to 350 degrees F.

5. In a mixing bowl, beat the cream cheese on medium speed until fluffy, about 2 minutes. Add 1 cup sugar. Beat 2 more minutes. Add eggs one at a time. Add 1 teaspoon vanilla. Spread mixture over pears.

6. Bake 50 minutes or until the top is set but still wobbles.

7. In a small bowl, mix sour cream with remaining sugar and vanilla. Pour over cheesecake and bake an additional 8 to 10 minutes.

8. Remove from oven and cool on a wire rack. Refrigerate at least 4 hours before serving.

9. When ready to serve, top with whipped cream.

NOTE

· Canned or bottled pears also work well for this recipe. Simply decrease roasting time to 10 minutes.

Garden Party

Cinnamon Bruschetta with Strawberry-Pineapple Relish

PREP AND COOKING TIME: 25 MIN · SERVES 12

FRUIT RELISH

1 cup fresh strawberries, diced small
1 cup pineapple, diced small

DRESSING

¼ cup lemon juice
1 teaspoon poppy seeds

½ cup honey
Pinch of salt

GLAZE

½ cup powdered sugar
1 teaspoon warm water

½ teaspoon ground cinnamon

12 slices sourdough or French bread baguette cut on a diagonal

Mint leaves for garnish (optional)
Balsamic glaze for garnish (optional)

1. In a medium-size bowl, combine strawberries, pineapple, lemon juice, honey, poppy seeds, and pinch of salt. Set aside.

2. In a small bowl, stir together powdered sugar, cinnamon, and water until glaze is the consistency of a royal icing.

3. Drizzle glaze on both sides of the sliced bread and place on a large cooking sheet lined with parchment paper.

4. Bake at 350 degrees F. for 10 minutes, turning bread over if necessary.

5. Let bread cool. When ready to serve, top bread with fruit relish. Garnish with mint leaves and balsamic glaze if desired.

VARIATIONS

- Change the flavor by using 2 cups of a variety of other fruits diced small: peaches, mangoes, kiwis, pomegranates, blueberries, or cherries.

He knew he *looked* the part of a gentleman worthy of taking a turn around a gathering with a lady as beautiful and refined as Miss Black, but he also knew she was miles above his touch.

THE LADY AND THE HIGHWAYMAN
Sarah M. Eden

Fruit Tart with an Apricot Glaze

PREP AND COOKING TIME: 1 HOUR 30 MIN
CHILL TIME: 2 HOURS (OR OVERNIGHT) · SERVES 6 TO 8

CRUST

1½ cups all-purpose flour

⅛ teaspoon salt

½ cup butter, room temperature

¼ cup granulated sugar

1 large egg, lightly beaten

FILLING

¼ cup granulated sugar

3 large egg yolks

2 tablespoons all-purpose flour

2 tablespoons cornstarch

1¼ cups whole milk

1 teaspoon vanilla extract

APRICOT GLAZE

½ cup apricot preserves or jam

1 tablespoon water

FRUIT

3 cups fruit (raspberries, strawberries, blueberries, blackberries, sliced mangoes, sliced peaches, kiwifruits, etc.)

1. **For the crust:** In a small bowl, whisk flour and salt. Set aside.

2. Using either a stand mixer or a hand mixer with a large bowl, cream butter and sugar until light and fluffy. Gradually add beaten egg, mixing until just incorporated. Add flour mixture and mix until just combined.

3. Form dough into a disc, then cover with plastic wrap and refrigerate for 15 to 30 minutes, or until firm. (Dough can also be placed in the freezer for 10 to 15 minutes.)

4. With a nonstick cooking spray, spray a 10-inch tart pan with a removable bottom. Spread chilled dough over the bottom and up the sides of the pan. Cover with plastic wrap and place in the freezer for 15 minutes.

5. Remove dough from the freezer and lightly prick the bottom of the crust with a fork. Place tart pan on a larger baking sheet and bake on the center rack of the oven for 5 minutes at 400 degrees F. Reduce oven temperature to 350 degrees F. and bake for another 15 to 20 minutes, or until lightly brown.

6. Remove crust from oven and place on a wire rack to cool completely before filling.

7. **For the filling:** In a medium-size heatproof bowl, whisk sugar and

She whispered against his lips what sounded like his name as her arms wrapped around his neck. He'd dreamed of this moment again and again over the months he'd known her. She'd claimed his heart from the beginning, and every day it became more irrevocably hers.

THE GENTLEMAN AND THE THIEF
Sarah M. Eden

CONTINUED ON PAGE 64

egg yolks together. Sift the flour and the cornstarch together, then add to the egg mixture, whisking together until smooth.

8. In a medium saucepan, bring milk just to boiling. (Milk will start to foam up.) Remove from heat and slowly add to egg mixture, whisking constantly to prevent curdling. (If egg does curdle, pour mixture through a strainer.)

9. Return mixture to saucepan and cook over medium heat until boiling, whisking constantly until it becomes thick. Stir in vanilla extract.

10. Pour mixture into a bowl and cover with plastic wrap to prevent a crust forming. Cool to room temperature.

11. **For the glaze:** In a small bowl, heat apricot preserves or jam and water in the microwave until melted, 1 to 2 minutes. Strain through a fine sieve to remove any lumps.

12. **To assemble the tart:** Gently place your hand under the tart pan, touching only the bottom and not the sides. The fluted tart ring will fall away and slide down your arm. To remove the tart from the bottom of the pan, run a knife or thin metal spatula between the crust and metal bottom, then slide the crust onto a serving platter.

13. Spread a thin layer of apricot glaze over the bottom and sides of the baked tart. Allow to dry for 20 to 25 minutes. Then spread the pastry cream onto the bottom of the tart shell.

14. Arrange fruit on top of the cream, starting at the outside edge and working toward the center of the tart. After fruit has been arranged, rewarm the glaze and gently brush a light coat over the fruit.

15. Serve immediately.

DID YOU KNOW? Victorian ladies'
clothes were often black because of the clouds
of pollution in the city. If a lady wore a
light-colored dress outside, it would be
gray by the time she returned home.

NOTES
- The baked crust can be covered and stored on the counter for up to 2 days.
- If you are not using the filling right away, it can be refrigerated in an airtight container until needed. Simply whisk filling before using to make smooth.
- This tart is best if eaten the same day it is assembled, but if not serving immediately, tart can be refrigerated for up to 2 days. Simply bring to room temperature before serving.

Victorian Games

CONSEQUENCES
For 4+ players

Requires paper, pens, and a flat surface to play on.

PREPARATION: Players sit around a table or in a circle. Each player begins with a sheet of paper and a pen.

HOW TO PLAY: Each player begins by writing a phrase or sentence at the top of their paper. This could be the beginning of a story, a description, or anything else they choose. Each player folds the top of the paper over to conceal what they've written, leaving only the last part of their phrase visible, then passes the paper to the person on their left.

The next player reads the visible phrase and continues the story by writing the next part. The player then folds the paper to conceal what they've written, leaving only the last part visible, and passes the paper to the next player. Players continue to write and pass the papers around the circle until each sheet of paper has been filled.

Once the papers have been returned to the original writers, each player unfolds their paper and takes a turn reading the completed stories aloud.

VARIATIONS TO THE GAME: Set a theme for the stories, impose a word limit on each turn, or allow players to illustrate their contributions.

IF YOU LOVE ME, DEAREST, SMILE!
For 4+ players

Players sit in a circle with one person designated as "It." That person is allowed to smile, laugh, tell jokes, make silly faces, or do whatever it takes to make everyone else laugh. The other players must keep a straight face, because once a player laughs or even smiles, they are out. The person who manages to keep a straight face the longest wins the game and becomes "It" for the next round. Get ready for loads of laughs, epic eye contact, and maybe even some playful flirtation!

Chilled Fruit Soups

CHILLED RASPBERRY SOUP

PREP AND COOKING TIME: 15 MIN · CHILL TIME: 1 HOUR · SERVES 6

4 cups fresh raspberries, washed

2 cups sour cream

1 cup milk

1 cup ginger ale

¼ cup granulated sugar

2 tablespoons orange juice

2 tablespoons lemon juice

1. In a blender, blend berries until smooth. Strain through a fine sieved strainer over a glass bowl to remove the seeds from the juice.
2. Whisk sour cream, milk, ginger ale, sugar, orange juice, and lemon juice with the fruit.
3. Cover and refrigerate until chilled, about 1 hour or overnight.
4. When ready to serve, ladle soup into bowls and garnish with fresh raspberries and a sprig of mint.

VARIATIONS

• This recipe can also be made with strawberries, blackberries, blueberries, or cherries.

CHILLED PEACH SOUP

PREP AND COOKING TIME: 15 MIN · CHILL TIME: OVERNIGHT · SERVES 6

3 cups frozen peaches, divided

1 cup whipping cream

2 cups milk

½ cup sour cream

granulated sugar to taste

1. In a blender, blend 2 cups frozen peaches, whipping cream, milk, and sour cream on high until smooth. Add sugar to taste. Chill overnight.
2. Blend remaining 1 cup of peaches on high until smooth. Keep frozen until ready to serve. Using a scoop, place peaches in individual serving bowls. Cover with chilled soup and garnish with a mint leaf.

A grin blossomed on the man's face, and blimey if it didn't fully upend her. Ginger men were often dismissed as less handsome, less striking, but bless him if he didn't prove that utterly and entirely false with a simple upward tip of his mouth.

THE MERCHANT AND THE ROGUE
Sarah M. Eden

Panzanella Salad

PREP TIME: 25 MIN · RESTING TIME: 25 MIN · SERVES 6

DRY BREAD

½ loaf rustic Italian bread, cut into 1-inch cubes

1 tablespoon extra-virgin olive oil

1 generous pinch of salt

DRESSING

2¼ pounds ripe tomatoes, cut into 1-inch pieces

¼ cup red wine vinegar

½ cup extra-virgin olive oil

2 cloves garlic, finely minced

½ teaspoon Dijon mustard

⅛ teaspoon black pepper

pinch of salt

2 small shallots, peeled and thinly sliced

½ cup fresh basil, thinly chopped

4 ounces shaved Romano cheese or fresh baby mozzarella

1. **For the bread:** In a large mixing bowl, combine bread, olive oil, and salt. Toss to coat bread (save bowl for later use). Spread the cubed bread on a large sheet pan and bake at 400 degrees F. for 10 minutes, or until golden brown. Bread should remain a bit chewy.

2. **For the dressing:** Place a colander over the mixing bowl. Place tomatoes in the colander and sprinkle with a pinch of salt. Toss with your hand. Set bowl aside for 5 minutes to allow tomatoes to release their juices.

3. Move colander to the sink to continue draining. In the bowl with the tomato juice, add red wine vinegar, olive oil, garlic, mustard, and black pepper. Whisk to combine.

4. Add tomatoes from the colander, bread cubes, shallots, basil, and cheese to the mixing bowl and toss to coat bread with the dressing.

5. Allow the salad to sit for 25 to 30 minutes.

6. When ready to serve, toss the salad one more time and transfer to a serving bowl or platter.

VARIATIONS

- Serve salad with grilled shrimp or chicken.
- In step 4, add diced plums, fresh corn cut off the cob, or fresh diced and peeled peaches for extra flavor.
- Increase the flavor by using an infused garlic or Tuscan herb olive oil in place of the extra-virgin olive oil or a Tuscan herb balsamic vinegar or plain balsamic vinegar for the dressing.

Baz crossed to her. He snaked an arm around her waist, then kissed her slowly and deeply. She hooked her arms around his neck and melted against him.

"You're beautiful, Gemma. Don't ever think otherwise."

THE BACHELOR AND THE BRIDE
Sarah M. Eden

He moved his hand tenderly until his fingertips grazed the back of her neck. Every strand of hair, every cell of her skin came alive at his touch.

She could not have said with any certainty who moved first or if they simply came together at the same moment, but when his lips touched hers, she felt the delicious sensation of simultaneously falling and floating. Her legs could no longer support her, but she felt as if she could never fall as long as he held her.

She reached her arms about his neck, returning pressure for pressure, tenderness for tenderness. As his arms wrapped solidly around her, she saw firelight behind her eyes, sparks of gold and blue, heat and warmth made visible by the touch of his mouth on hers.

Had anything ever felt so lovely, so perfect?

THE ART OF LOVE AND LIES
Rebecca Anderson

Classic Carrot Cake

PREP AND COOKING TIME: 1 HOUR 20 MIN · SERVES 15 TO 20

CAKE

2½ cups all-purpose flour

1 teaspoon salt

1 teaspoon ground cinnamon

1 teaspoon baking soda

1 cup vegetable or canola oil

2 cups granulated sugar

3 large eggs

2 teaspoons vanilla extract

2 cups grated carrots

1 cup crushed pineapple, drained

1 cup chopped pecans or walnuts, toasted if desired, plus ¼ cup for garnish

FROSTING

8 ounces cream cheese, softened

½ cup butter

2 cups powdered sugar

1 teaspoon vanilla extract

1. **For the cake:** In a large mixing bowl, combine flour, salt, cinnamon, and baking soda.

2. Using either a stand mixer or a hand mixer with a large bowl, beat together oil, sugar, eggs, and vanilla until blended.

3. Add the flour mixture to the egg mixture. Mix until combined.

4. Fold in grated carrots, pineapple, and nuts using a rubber spatula.

5. Pour batter into a greased and floured 9x13-inch metal cake pan. (Make sure the sides of the cake pan are at least 2 inches tall.) Bake at 350 degrees F. for 55 to 60 minutes, or until cake tester comes out clean. Cool completely on a wire rack.

6. **For the frosting:** Using either a stand mixer or a hand mixer with a large bowl, beat the cream cheese until smooth. Add butter and mix for about 30 to 60 seconds, or until smooth.

7. Add powdered sugar and vanilla extract and continue mixing until fully combined. Stop and scrape down the sides of the bowl as needed.

8. Frost cooled cake and garnish with toasted nuts.

In walked a woman he knew immediately: Móirín Donnelly. She was proud, confident, and spitting daggers as usual when her eyes settled on him. She was also, without question, the most strikingly beautiful woman he'd ever known.

THE QUEEN AND THE KNAVE
Sarah M. Eden

Dinner Party

Crustless Shepherd's Pie

PREP AND COOKING TIME: 1 HOUR 5 MIN TO 1 HOUR 30 MIN
SERVES 8 TO 12

FILLING

2 tablespoons coconut oil

1 cup chopped onion

2 cloves garlic, minced

1 pound ground beef or ground turkey

2 teaspoons dried parsley

1 teaspoon dried rosemary

1 teaspoon dried thyme

½ teaspoon salt

½ teaspoon pepper

1 (15-ounce) can crushed tomatoes

½ cup beef broth

1 cup frozen peas and carrots, or vegetable medley

1 cup frozen corn

1 teaspoon Worcestershire sauce

POTATO TOPPING

2 to 3 large potatoes, peeled and cut into bite-size pieces

8 tablespoons unsalted butter

⅓ cup half-and-half

½ teaspoon garlic powder

½ teaspoon salt

¼ teaspoon pepper

¼ cup Parmesan cheese

He was a handsome man [with] blue eyes that were mesmerizing in their brilliant sparkle. Right now those eyes danced just looking at her, and she knew that to him she was the only woman of any notice here tonight.

THE LADY OF THE LAKES
Josi S. Kilpack

1. **For the filling:** In a large skillet, heat oil over medium-high heat. Add onion and garlic. Cook for 2 to 3 minutes or until onion is translucent.

2. Reduce heat to medium and add ground beef. Cook for 8 to 10 minutes until brown.

3. Add parsley, rosemary, thyme, salt, and pepper. Stir well.

4. Add Worcestershire sauce.

5. Add tomatoes. Stir well.

6. Add broth and frozen vegetables. Simmer for 5 to 10 minutes.

7. Turn off heat, cover skillet, and set aside.

8. **For the topping:** In a large stock pot, cover potatoes with water. Bring to a boil, then reduce heat to a simmer. Cook for 10 to 15 minutes or until potatoes are tender.

9. Drain potatoes and return to pot.

10. Add butter, half-and-half, garlic powder, salt, and pepper. Mash potatoes until all the ingredients are mixed well. Stir in Parmesan cheese.

VICTORIAN: Dinner Party

IF USING A DEEP-DISH, 9-INCH PIE PLATE:

1. Lightly grease pie plate with nonstick cooking spray.
2. Spread filling evenly in the pie plate and cover with potato topping.
3. Place on a baking sheet. (The juice tends to boil over.)
4. Bake uncovered at 400 degrees F. for 25 to 30 minutes.
5. Cool 15 minutes and serve.

IF USING MUFFIN TINS FOR INDIVIDUAL SERVINGS:

1. Line muffin tins with paper liners.
2. Layer 2 tablespoons of filling in each tin. Cover with potato topping.
3. Bake at 350 degrees F. for 20 to 25 minutes.
4. Cool 10 minutes and serve.

DID YOU KNOW? The Victorian era is known for the Industrial Revolution and the beginnings of social reform, including advancements in education, public health, and women's rights.

NOTES
- For a thicker consistency in the filling, use 2 tablespoons tomato paste instead of crushed tomatoes.
- For a faster preparation of the topping, use instant potatoes.

Roast Beef Dinner

PREP AND COOKING TIME: 2 HOURS 30 MIN · SERVES 6 TO 8

2 teaspoons coconut oil

4 pounds boneless chuck roast (or pork roast)

1 onion, chopped

2 cloves garlic, minced

2 bay leaves

1 teaspoon salt

½ teaspoon black pepper

1 pound potatoes, chopped into bite-size pieces

1 pound carrots, chopped into bite-size pieces

1. Place a Dutch oven on the stovetop. Add oil and heat on high 10 to 15 minutes until it smokes. Sear meat in the center of the pan 1 minute on each side. (The hotter the oil, the crispier the skin.)

2. Remove pan from heat. Remove meat and set aside.

3. In the hot Dutch oven, arrange the onion, garlic, and bay leaves on the bottom. Sprinkle with salt and pepper. Return meat to Dutch oven.

4. Arrange potatoes and carrots around the meat. Cover.

5. Cook in the oven at 325 degrees F. for 30 minutes.

6. Reduce heat to 300 degrees F. and cook for an additional 90 minutes, or until meat is tender and the thermometer reads 145 degrees F. at thickest part of the roast.

7. Transfer roast to a platter and let it rest for 10 to 15 minutes before slicing and serving.

Hyacinth felt more firmly aware of her fingers where they touched him, of her thoughts, of her surroundings. It was as though this small connection to Lucas Harding made the entire world more clear.

THE ORCHIDS OF ASHTHORNE HALL
Rebecca Anderson

NOTE
· This recipe can be made in a slow cooker. After searing the meat in a skillet, place all ingredients in a large slow cooker. Cook on low for 6 hours.
· Save the drippings from the roast to use in the Yorkshire Pudding.

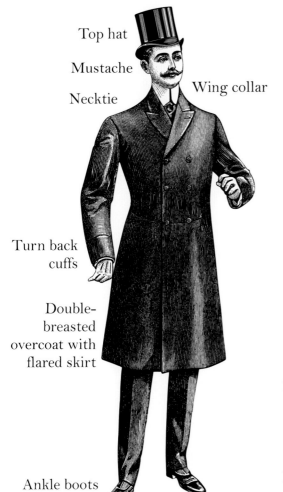

Fashion of the Day

1837 to 1901

Top hat

Mustache

Necktie

Wing collar

Turn back cuffs

Double-breasted overcoat with flared skirt

Ankle boots

Bangs

High collar

Brooch

Fitted top

Puff sleeves

Gloves

Low waist

Bustle

Ruffle skirt or flared skirt

Yorkshire Pudding

PREP AND COOKING TIME: 25 MIN · CHILL TIME: 1 HOUR · MAKES 12

1 cup flour

1 teaspoon sea salt

3 large eggs

1¼ cups whole milk (or half-and-half)

4 tablespoons sunflower oil or coconut oil

1. Add flour and salt to a small mixing bowl. Set aside.
2. In a separate bowl, whisk eggs and milk together.
3. Slowly add flour mixture to egg mixture and whisk until smooth.
4. Cover bowl with plastic wrap or lid and chill in the refrigerator for 1 hour.
5. Add a teaspoon of oil to the bottom of each cup of a muffin tin. Heat at 425 degrees F. for 10 minutes.
6. Remove muffin tin from the oven. (Be careful—both the pan and the oil will be very hot!)
7. Scoop ¼ cup chilled batter into each cup.
8. Return muffin tin to the oven and cook an additional 20 minutes, or until pudding is golden-brown.
9. Serve immediately.

VARIATION

- Toad in the Hole: Mix ¼-pound cooked sausage into batter during step 3.

They shared stories of their childhoods and parents, spoke of their hopes for their futures. They found in each other a kinship that went beyond their currently shared difficulties, a companionship they grew increasingly reluctant to even imagine losing.

The Governess and the Fugitive, THE COMPLETE PENNY DREADFUL COLLECTION
Sarah M. Eden

NOTES

- Traditionally, beef drippings were used instead of oil. If you saved the drippings from your roast, the fat flavors the pudding deliciously!
- This dish can be served by itself or with gravy.

VICTORIAN: Dinner Party

Mixed Berry Trifle

PREP AND COOKING TIME: 1 HOUR
CHILL TIME: 1 HOUR (OR OVERNIGHT) · SERVES 10 TO 12

ANGEL FOOD CAKE

¾ cup + 2 tablespoons all-purpose flour (or 1 cup cake flour)

1¼ cups powdered sugar

1½ cups egg whites (10 to 12 large eggs, room temperature)

1½ teaspoons cream of tartar

1½ teaspoons vanilla extract

¼ teaspoon salt

1 cup granulated sugar

FILLING

16 ounces cream cheese, softened

1 cup sour cream

1 teaspoon vanilla extract

1½ teaspoons almond extract

1 cup powdered sugar

½ cup whipping cream

2 bags (16-ounces) mixed berry fruit, frozen

1. **For the cake:** In a medium-size bowl, whisk together flour and powdered sugar. Set aside.

2. Using a stand mixer or a hand mixer with a large bowl, combine egg whites, cream of tartar, vanilla extract, and salt. Mix well.

3. With mixer on high, beat in sugar one tablespoon at a time, adding more only once the previous sugar has been dissolved, about every 15 seconds. (Do not scrape the sides of the bowl during mixing.)

4. Beat until stiff peaks form. The mixture will be thickened, glossy, and sticky and will have considerably increased in volume.

5. Using a rubber spatula, gently fold flour into sugar mixture, about ½ cup at a time, until just combined. Do not overmix.

6. Spread evenly into an ungreased, 10-inch tube pan. Use a knife or spatula to cut through the batter and break through any air bubbles.

7. Bake on the center rack of the oven at 375 degrees F. for 35 minutes, or until the top of the cake springs back when lightly touched. Any cracks on the surface should look dry.

8. Immediately invert cake onto a wire rack, leaving it in the pan to cool thoroughly.

9. Once cake has cooled, use a serrated knife to carefully loosen sides of cake from pan. Cut cake into 1-inch cubes.

10. **For the filling:** Using a hand mixer with a large bowl, beat cream cheese until smooth. Mix in sour cream, vanilla, and almond extract. Add powdered sugar and mix until combined.

11. Whip ½ cup whipping cream. Fold gently into cream cheese mixture. Set aside.

She wore a formal gown he'd never seen her in before. The beautiful shade of blue was the perfect complement to her complexion and hair. Her high cheekbones and green eyes were accentuated by an artful hair arrangement, and she was exquisite.

PROTECTING
HER HEART
Nancy Campbell Allen

CONTINUED ON PAGE 81

12. **To assemble the cake:** Layer half of the angel food cake cubes in a clear trifle bowl. Top with half of the berries, and then layer half of the filling. Repeat for second layer.

13. Cover with plastic wrap and refrigerate trifle for 1 hour or overnight until ready to be served.

VARIATIONS

- This trifle can also be made with just frozen raspberries or strawberries. It also layers beautifully in individual small mason jars or small glass bowls.

DID YOU KNOW? Historically, both men and women wore corsets, though by the mid-1800s, men's corsets had fallen out of fashion.

NOTES

- Egg whites sold in a carton will not usually whip properly, so use fresh eggs. When cracking eggs, make sure the bowl is grease-free and completely clean. Crack each egg into a smaller bowl and then transfer egg white to the measuring cup. The egg whites must be completely free of any yolk to ensure a stiff peak.
- The filling can be doubled to make two trifles. It is sweet enough that the berries do not need sugar.
- To save time, use a prepared angel food cake or pound cake.

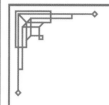
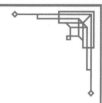

STEAMPUNK

BRITISH STEAMPUNK is a fictional era that blends the elegance of the Victorian era with imaginative steam-powered technology, creating a world of romance and adventure. Amidst the cobblestone streets and gaslit alleys of an alternate nineteenth-century Britain, airships float gracefully through the smoggy skies, and intricate clockwork devices bring a touch of magic to everyday life. Gentlemen adorned in waistcoats and goggles and ladies in corseted gowns with gears and lace navigate a society where love and innovation intertwine. Against the backdrop of brass and steam, hearts ignite in clandestine workshops and atop grand mechanical marvels, crafting timeless tales of passion and ingenuity in a world where anything is possible.

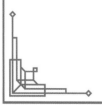
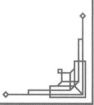

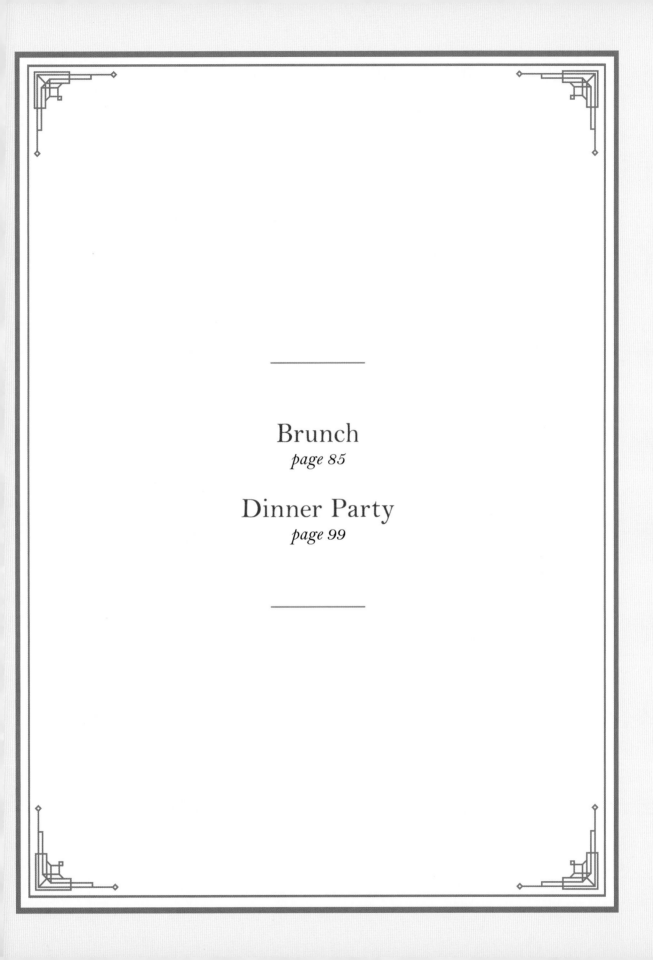

Brunch
page 85

Dinner Party
page 99

Brunch

Mocktails

MINT CORDIAL

PREP TIME: 10 MIN · STEEP TIME: 24 HOURS · SERVES 2

2¾ cups water

4½ cups granulated sugar

1 small lemon, sliced

1 orange, sliced

1 teaspoon orange zest

½ cup fresh mint leaves

12 ounces sparkling water or club soda

1. In a saucepan over medium-high heat, bring water to a boil. Add sugar and stir until dissolved. Increase heat to high and bring syrup to a boil. Remove from heat and set aside.

2. Add lemon and orange slices, orange zest, and mint leaves to syrup.

3. Cover and let mixture sit on kitchen counter for 24 hours.

4. When ready to serve, strain mixture into a 16-ounce bottle or pitcher until three-quarters full.

5. Mix with chilled sparkling water and garnish with fresh mint leaves.

SANGRIA SPLASH

PREP TIME: 5 MIN · CHILL TIME: 2 HOURS · SERVES 6

1 lemon, sliced

1 orange, sliced

1 apple, sliced

1 cinnamon stick

1 teaspoon whole cloves

1 cup grape juice

4 cups sparkling or flat water

1. In a large pitcher, mix lemon, orange, apple, cinnamon stick, cloves, and grape juice.

2. Refrigerate at least 2 hours.

3. Strain the juice into glasses until three-quarters full.

4. Add sparkling water. Serve cold.

NOTE
· The longer the punch sits, the stronger the flavor will be.

CONTINUED ON NEXT PAGE

My fairy godmother was all talk and no action. Like the tooth fairy, she was definitely not someone I could depend on. I had a sneaking suspicion the two had run off together a long time ago and were now downing drinks with umbrellas while they lounged on a beach somewhere exotic and peaceful.

GLASS SLIPPERS, EVER AFTER, AND ME
Julie Wright

STEAMPUNK: Brunch

CHERRY SHIRLEY TEMPLE

PREP TIME: 10 MIN · CHILL TIME: 30 MIN · SERVES 4

4 tablespoons fresh lemon juice

4 tablespoons granulated sugar

32 ounces ginger ale

12 tablespoons tart cherry juice

8 tablespoons freshly squeezed orange juice

1 jar maraschino cherries

1. Chill individual glasses in the refrigerator for 30 minutes.

2. Juice lemon onto a shallow plate.

3. On a separate plate, spread out sugar in an even layer.

4. Dip the rim of the chilled glass in the lemon juice, then in the sugar. (The sugar should stick to the rim of the glass.)

5. Add ginger ale, cherry juice, and orange juice. Mix well.

6. Garnish with 2 maraschino cherries and serve.

SUMMER SLUSH

PREP TIME: 15 MIN · FREEZE TIME: 2 HOURS · SERVES 12

2 (6-ounce) cans frozen orange juice, thawed

1 (46-ounce) can pineapple juice

1 tablespoon lemon juice

1 tablespoon coconut-flavored syrup

1 (2-liter) bottle sparking water or club soda

1. In a large bowl, mix all ingredients except the sparkling water.

2. Divide mixture evenly into three (1-gallon) freezer bags.

3. Freeze at least 2 hours.

4. When ready to serve, place the frozen drink mix into a large punch bowl. Add the sparking water. Using a wooden spoon, break up the frozen drink mixture.

A History of Steampunk

The term *steampunk* was coined in the 1980s by science-fiction author K. W. Jeter to describe adventurous stories set in an alternate nineteenth-century Britain or the American West that embrace the mood and imagination of the classic science fiction writers of the Victorian era. Steampunk stories incorporate retrofuturistic technology inspired by the Industrial Revolution where steam power is in use, and they often use alternative-history-style technology like steam cannons, ray guns, lighter-than-air ships, analog computers, or automatons.

Steampunk aesthetic is filled with complicated gears and cogs intertwined with clockwork pieces and with polished brass or leather fittings. The fashion tends to include feathered top hats, aviation goggles, corsets, vests, gloves, and boots. Often the clothes are adorned with mechanical elements as well.

NOTABLE VICTORIAN-ERA SCIENCE FICTION NOVELS

Frankenstein: or, The Modern Prometheus by Mary Shelley (1818)
The Last Man by Mary Shelley (1826)
Some Words with a Mummy by Edgar Allan Poe (1845)
Journey to the Center of the Earth by Jules Verne (1864)
The Steam Man of the Prairies by Edward S. Ellis (1868)
Twenty Thousand Leagues Under the Sea by Jules Verne (1870)
Around the World in Eighty Days by Jules Verne (1872)
The Time Machine by H. G. Wells (1895)
The Island of Doctor Moreau by H. G. Wells (1896)
The War of the Worlds by H. G. Wells (1898)

Victorian Baked Eggs

PREP AND COOKING TIME: 30 MIN · SERVES 1

1 English muffin, toasted

¼ cup finely chopped ham (bacon, Canadian bacon, or sausage, fully cooked)

2 tablespoons shredded Gruyère cheese, divided

2 tablespoons whipping cream

2 eggs

pinch of fresh chives (or parsley, dill, or rosemary)

pinch of salt and pepper

1. Preheat oven to 375 degrees F.
2. Place cupcake liner in muffin tin.
3. If using ramekins, brush olive oil on the bottom and sides.
4. Tear half of a toasted English muffin into small pieces and layer on the bottom of a lined muffin tin cup.
5. Add layer of ham and sprinkle with half of the cheese. Add cream.
6. Crack eggs over ham mixture.
7. Top with remaining cheese along with fresh chives. Add pinch of salt and pepper.
8. Bake at 375 degrees F. 15 to 20 minutes, or until egg whites are just set with the yokes still runny.
9. Remove from oven and let sit for 2 to 3 minutes.
10. Serve with the remaining half of the toasted English muffin.

VARIATION

- For a gluten-free version of this recipe, omit the English muffin, or use a gluten-free muffin.

He should have kissed her when he'd had the chance—that night they'd danced behind the mast. Each morning when he awoke to her standing above him with breakfast, he regretted his forbearance.

GEORGANA'S SECRET
Arlem Hawks

NOTE

- If using a muffin tin, line cups with either heavy-duty cupcake liners or 2 regular cupcake liners. If using an individual 8-ounce ramekin, brush olive oil on the bottom and sides before filling.

Burrata Salad

PREP AND COOKING TIME: 10 MIN · SERVES 4

DRESSING

3 tablespoons extra-virgin olive oil

1 large lemon, juiced

Salt and black pepper to taste

SALAD

6 ounces baby arugula or spring mix

6 ounces fresh strawberries

6 ounces fresh raspberries

6 ounces fresh blackberries

1 small shallot, halved and sliced

4 ounces burrata cheese

1. In a small bowl, whisk together olive oil, lemon juice, salt, and pepper.

2. In a large mixing bowl, add arugula, berries, and shallots.

3. When ready to serve, top salad with dressing and gently toss. Transfer to a serving platter and top with burrata.

VARIATIONS

- Use an infused lemon olive oil and balsamic instead of the dressing.
- Add pistachios with the berries to provide a nice crunch.
- Easily swap out seasonal fruit for blueberries, peaches, or cherries.
- Instead of fruit, add 1 sliced avocado and 1 cup sliced cherry tomatoes.

Daniel pulled her closer to his chest, and she put her arms around his head and neck. This was heaven, her heaven.

KISS OF THE SPINDLE
Nancy Campbell Allen

Almond Bakewell Tart

PREP AND COOKING TIME: 1 HOUR 30 MIN
CHILL TIME: 30 MIN • SERVES 12

CRUST

2 cups all-purpose flour

2 tablespoons granulated sugar

½ teaspoon salt

½ cup butter, frozen

2 large egg yolks

½ teaspoon almond extract

1 to 2 tablespoons cold water

FRANGIPANE

9 tablespoons butter, room temperature

1 cup + 2 tablespoons powdered sugar

3 large eggs, room temperature

½ teaspoon almond extract

1⅓ cups almond meal

¼ cup all-purpose flour

1 cup cherry jam

½ cup slivered almonds

2 tablespoons powdered sugar

He had wanted to kiss her forever. Her response was equally passionate and unrestrained but somehow even better than he could have imagined.

BRASS CARRIAGES AND GLASS HEARTS
Nancy Campbell Allen

1. **For the crust:** In a large bowl, mix flour, granulated sugar, and salt. Grate frozen butter into the mixture and rub the butter into the flour using a pastry cutter or your fingers until the mixture resembles coarse crumbs.

2. In a separate bowl, beat the egg yolks lightly with the almond extract. Stir into the flour mixture. Continue mixing while adding just enough water to form a sticky dough.

3. Roll out dough on a lightly floured surface to ¼-inch thickness. Transfer dough to a 9-inch tart pan, pressing along the sides and trimming any excess dough. Refrigerate dough for 30 minutes.

4. Line the top of dough with parchment paper and fill with pie weights or dried beans. Blind-bake the crust at 400 degrees F. for 10 minutes. Remove pie weights and parchment and bake an additional 5 minutes, or until crust is barely golden-brown. Set aside to cool.

5. **For the frangipane:** Cream together butter and powdered sugar with a mixer on medium speed 1 minute or until light and fluffy. Add eggs one at a time, beating well after each one. Add the almond extract and beat for an additional 30 seconds. Spoon in the almond meal and flour while the mixer is running and combine well.

6. **To assemble the tart:** Spread jam evenly along the crust. Top with the frangipane, spreading over tart until smooth.

7. Bake at 375 degrees F. for 20 minutes. Remove tart from oven and scatter almonds across the top. Bake an additional 5 to 10 minutes, or until golden brown and a tester inserted into the center of the tart comes out clean.

STEAMPUNK: Brunch

8. Dust with additional powdered sugar.

9. Serve slightly warm, or at room temperature.

VARIATION
• Use raspberry or strawberry jam instead of cherry jam.

DID YOU KNOW? Steampunk jewelry often incorporates nautical or oceanic themes like portholes or an octopus as a nod to *Twenty Thousand Leagues Under the Sea* by Jules Verne.

NOTES
• Scrunching the parchment paper into a wad helps it stay in the pan during the blind baking.
• Baked tart can be stored at room temperature in an airtight container for up to 3 days.

Citrus Olive Oil Cake

PREP AND COOKING TIME: 50 MIN · SERVES 8

⅔ cup granulated sugar

½ teaspoon baking powder

¼ teaspoon baking soda

¼ teaspoon salt

1¼ cup all-purpose flour

⅔ cup olive oil

½ cup plain Greek yogurt

2 large eggs

3 tablespoons lemon juice

Zest of 1 lemon

powdered sugar

whipping cream (optional)

fresh fruit or berry compote (optional)

1. In a large bowl, mix sugar, baking powder, baking soda, salt, and flour together.

2. In a separate bowl, combine olive oil, Greek yogurt, and eggs. Slowly whisk egg mixture into the flour mixture.

3. Add lemon juice and lemon zest. Stir until completely combined.

4. Pour batter into greased 9-inch round pan. Bake at 350 degrees F. for 30 to 35 minutes or until a toothpick inserted in the center comes out clean.

5. Cool 10 minutes before slicing.

6. When ready to serve, sprinkle powdered sugar on top. Add dollop of whipping cream and fresh fruit or berry compote, if desired.

VARIATION

• For added flavor, use an infused lemon or orange olive oil.

Marie turned when she saw Jonathan's reflection in the window. He crossed the room to her with a smile, and she felt her heavy mood lift. He was dashing with his dark hair and his poet's soul, and he smiled as he placed a kiss on her cheek.

**Marie's Story,
BEAUTY AND
THE CLOCKWORK
BEAST**
Nancy Campbell Allen

NOTES

• Store cake in an airtight container for up to 4 days.

• This cake can be made early and kept in a freezer-safe container for up to 3 months. Double wrap cake in plastic wrap and aluminum foil. Thaw cake in refrigerator overnight before serving.

Dinner Party

Twice-Baked Potato Casserole

PREP AND COOKING TIME: 50 MIN · SERVES 10

POTATOES

6 medium russet potatoes (3½- to 4-pounds), peeled, baked, or boiled

⅔ cup sour cream

4 ounces cream cheese, softened

¼ cup butter

½ cup milk

2 cups cheddar cheese, shredded

10 slices bacon, cooked and crumbled

1 tablespoon fresh parsley

2 green onions, thinly sliced

½ teaspoon garlic powder

salt and pepper to taste

TOPPING

½ cup cheddar cheese, shredded

2 slices bacon, cooked and chopped

1 green onion, sliced

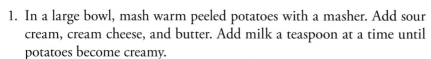

1. In a large bowl, mash warm peeled potatoes with a masher. Add sour cream, cream cheese, and butter. Add milk a teaspoon at a time until potatoes become creamy.

2. Mix in remaining ingredients and place in a 2-quart casserole dish.

3. Sprinkle with the toppings and bake at 375 degrees F. for 25 to 35 minutes or until cheese is melted and potatoes are heated through.

Her dark hair hung around her shoulders and framed her face in curls he knew firsthand to be softer than satin. Her deep, cobalt eyes locked with his, and he felt his mouth go dry.

BEAUTY AND THE CLOCKWORK BEAST
Nancy Campbell Allen

STEAMPUNK: Dinner Party

NOTE

· This casserole can be made early and baked the next day. Make potato mixture and place in casserole dish. Do not add any toppings. Cover dish and refrigerate overnight. When ready to serve, bake casserole covered at 325 degrees F. for 25 to 30 minutes. Remove from oven, stir, and then add toppings. Increase oven temperature to 375 degrees F. and bake uncovered for 15 to 20 minutes or until potatoes are heated through.

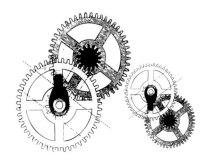

Steampunk Fashion

Adding a touch of steampunk flair to your wardrobe is easy.

- Common colors include brown, rust, and gold. Highlighting colors are often dark red, maroon, olive green, and yellow. Black and gray add a more industrialized look to the outfit.
- Add leather accents to a hat, vest, or boots or carry a leather over-the-shoulder bag.
- Accessorize a bowler or top hat with mechanical gears, keys, or feathers.
- Trim sleeves, collars, or gloves with lace or ruffles.
- Choose pinstripes as a pattern for pants or a vest.
- Attach a pocket watch to a bag or a belt.
- Corsets and bustle skirts are standard for women's wear, while men typically wear a three-piece suit consisting of a jacket, waistcoat, and pants.

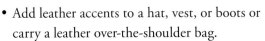

Mahi Mahi with Lemon Pepper Butter

PREP AND COOKING TIME: 25 MIN · SERVES 4

MAHI MAHI

4 (6-ounce) mahi mahi fillets

extra-virgin olive oil

salt and pepper to taste

LEMON-PEPPER BUTTER

2 ounces butter, softened

¾ teaspoon lemon pepper

¼ teaspoon salt

1 medium lemon, zested

1 tablespoon fresh Italian parsley, chopped

1. **For the mahi mahi:** Place mahi mahi on a large baking sheet lined with parchment paper.

2. Drizzle with olive oil and season with salt and pepper.

3. Bake at 450 degrees F. for 12 to 18 minutes or until fish is opaque and flakes easily.

4. **For the lemon-pepper butter:** In a small bowl, mix butter, lemon pepper, salt, lemon zest, and chopped parsley until combined.

5. Brush over baked fish and serve.

VARIATIONS

- For the mahi mahi, use an infused dill, lemon, or lime olive oil for extra flavor.
- Instead of lemon-pepper butter, make an aioli by mixing 2 tablespoons mayonnaise, 1 tablespoon extra-virgin olive oil, 2 cloves garlic, pressed, and salt and pepper to taste until combined. Serve on the side or on top of fish.
- For cod, bake at 400 degrees F. for 12 to 15 minutes.
- For trout, bake at 400 degrees F. in lightly greased foil packets for 10 to 15 minutes.

His face was so close to hers, and with her arm slung comfortably around his shoulders, she felt a joy she didn't think she'd ever had. An unfettered, excited, tumultuous feeling.

KISS OF THE SPINDLE
Nancy Campbell Allen

Baked Lemon Salmon

PREP AND COOKING TIME: 25 MIN · SERVES 4

4 (6-ounce) salmon fillets

salt and pepper to taste

2 tablespoons olive oil

1 teaspoon lemon pepper

1 medium lemon, halved

fresh parsley or dill (optional)

1. Place salmon on a large baking sheet lined with parchment paper. Season with salt and pepper.

2. In a small bowl, whisk together olive oil, lemon pepper, and juice of ½ lemon.

3. Spoon mixture over salmon, making sure both tops and sides are covered.

4. Thinly slice remaining ½ lemon and top each piece of salmon with a slice of lemon.

5. Bake at 400 degrees F. for 12 to 15 minutes, or until salmon is opaque and flaky when pulled apart with a fork.

6. Garnish with fresh parsley or dill.

He was so much more than merely handsome to Hazel. He was funny and kind and intelligent. He brightened the energy in the room, drew others to him as moths to a flame.

THE LADY IN THE COPPERGATE TOWER
Nancy Campbell Allen

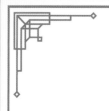

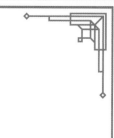

Lucy fought to keep her eyes from drifting shut at the sensation of his hand upon the small of her back. She had known from the moment he approached that she would dance with him. This close, he smelled of something wonderful, something she couldn't define, something that made her want to nuzzle her nose against his neck, kiss away the scar.

With a fair amount of alarm, she squelched the idea and focused on keeping her footing. She hadn't lied—she was a very good dancer. She was also fairly accomplished at the pianoforte, the harp, and the violin. She sewed in beautiful, neat stitches and was quite exceptional with a drawing pen and sketchbook. She had been gifted with an intelligent brain and a quick wit. She conversed well with people from all walks of life and could play a mean game of croquet.

What Lucy had never experienced, however, was a prolonged exchange with a man of substance, one whose personality seemed a match for her own. Boys, she handled well enough. She flirted easily and could entertain their interests on a surface level. But she had yet to feel the thrill of a genuine challenge for a man who played at a deeper and much more dangerous game.

This man was not a boy.

BEAUTY AND THE CLOCKWORK BEAST
Nancy Campbell Allen

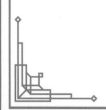
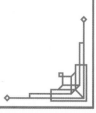

Beef Stroganoff

PREP AND COOKING TIME: 30 TO 40 MIN · SERVES 4 TO 6

1 pound ground beef

1½ cups beef broth

1 tablespoon Worcestershire sauce

1 medium onion, sliced into rings

1 small clove garlic, minced

1 teaspoon salt

1 cup sour cream

3 cups sliced mushrooms

1 (12-ounce) package extra-wide egg noodles

1. In a large skillet over medium-high heat, cook ground beef until brown. Drain. Return to skillet.

2. Add broth and Worcestershire sauce. Simmer over low heat for 5 to 10 minutes.

3. Add onion, garlic, and salt. Cook for 5 to 10 minutes until onion is translucent.

4. Add sour cream and mushrooms. Cover and simmer 10 minutes.

5. Following the directions on the package, cook egg noodles.

6. Add to beef mixture, stir well, and serve.

Calvin leaned in to kiss her full lips as the night's argument slipped away. When he lifted his head, Hattie put her hand behind his neck and pulled him back for an answering kiss of her own.

ALL THAT MAKES LIFE BRIGHT
Josi S. Kilpack

> DID YOU KNOW? In addition to steampunk, there are other fiction styles that embrace the "punk" label, including biopunk, clockpunk, cyberpunk, and dieselpunk.

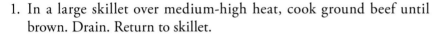

Flourless Chocolate Cake

PREP AND COOKING TIME: 1 HOUR 30 MIN
SET TIME: 1 HOUR 30 MIN • SERVES 12

CAKE

½ cup butter

1 cup semisweet chocolate chips

¾ cup granulated sugar

¼ teaspoon salt

1 teaspoon vanilla extract

3 large eggs

½ cup cocoa powder

GANACHE

½ cup heavy whipping cream

1 cup semisweet chocolate chips

1. **For the cake:** In a microwave-safe bowl, add butter and chocolate chips. Heat in 20-second intervals until butter melts and chocolate chips are soft. Stir after each interval until chips melt. Reheat if necessary.

2. Stir in sugar, salt, and vanilla.

3. Add eggs, whisking until smooth. Add cocoa powder and mix to combine.

4. Pour batter into a lightly greased 8-inch round cake pan lined with parchment paper.

5. Bake at 375 degrees F. for 25 minutes.

6. Remove cake from oven and cool in the pan for 5 minutes.

7. Loosen the cake from the edges of the pan with a knife and invert pan onto a serving plate. (The top will now be the bottom of the cake.) Allow cake to cool completely before topping with ganache.

8. **For the ganache:** Pour heavy whipping cream into a microwave-safe bowl or glass measuring cup and heat for 45 seconds to 1 minute. Add chocolate and let mixture sit for 2 minutes. Start whisking slowly in the middle of the bowl and continue until mixture is smooth and combined.

9. Spread ganache over the cake. (If you want it to drip chocolate over the edges, that is fine.) Allow ganache to set for several hours before serving.

VARIATIONS

• This cake can also be garnished with ¼ cup of toasted sliced almonds and 2 cups fresh raspberries or sliced strawberries. Sprinkle with powdered sugar if desired.

• Serve with whipping cream or a scoop of vanilla ice cream.

> "I don't think I can navigate all the unknowns of a seventeenth-century dinner party without people noticing my mistakes. The last thing I'd want to do is draw extra attention, but between not knowing the right etiquette or vocabulary, I'd be a walking disaster."

A TIME TRAVELER'S MASQUERADE
Sian Ann Bessey

AMERICAN WEST

THE AMERICAN WEST—a land of vast, untamed beauty and rugged landscapes—sets the stage for romance and adventure. Under the expansive skies with sunsets painting the horizon in hues of gold and crimson, cowboys and pioneers traverse the open plains and towering mountains. In this world of dusty trails and frontier towns, love blossoms amidst the hardships and simplicity of life. Gentlemen, with their weathered hats and steadfast gazes, court spirited ladies in flowing prairie dresses. Against the backdrop of campfires and starlit nights, hearts intertwine in a dance of passion and resilience, creating timeless tales of enduring love and boundless dreams.

Breakfast

Crustless Quiche

PREP AND COOKING TIME: 1 HOUR 15 MIN · SERVES 6 TO 8

5 eggs

½ cup half-and-half or whole milk

¼ teaspoon cumin

¼ teaspoon smoked paprika

¼ teaspoon salt

¼ teaspoon pepper

pinch of chili pepper (optional)

1 (4-ounce) can of green chilies, divided

2 cups shredded cheddar cheese, divided

4 corn tortillas, divided

salsa

guacamole

1. In a mixing bowl, combine eggs, half-and-half, cumin, smoked paprika, salt, pepper, and a pinch of chili pepper. Mix well and set aside.

2. Spray a 9-inch pie pan with olive oil or nonstick cooking spray. Spread half of the green chilis over the bottom of the dish. (They will not cover the entire bottom.)

3. Cover chilis with 2 tortillas cut into four triangles.

4. Spread 1 cup cheese on top of tortillas.

5. Repeat with a second layer of chilis, tortillas, and cheese.

6. Pour egg mixture over the top.

7. Sprinkle with paprika if desired.

8. Cook at 350 degrees F. for 35 to 40 minutes or until a knife inserted in the center comes out clean.

9. Cool 10 minutes, then serve with salsa and guacamole.

DID YOU KNOW? In 1856, the US Camel Corps was established in Texas with sixty-six camels imported from the Middle East. After the American Civil War, the camels were either sold or escaped into the wild.

NOTES
- Individual quiches can be made in ramekins or in muffin tins, filling two-thirds of the way full. Bake at 335 degrees F. for 25 to 30 minutes.
- This dish can be made the night before, refrigerated, and cooked in the morning.

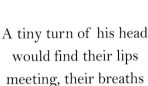

A tiny turn of his head would find their lips meeting, their breaths mingling. One slight adjustment. One small movement. It would be the easiest thing in all the world.

THE SHERIFFS OF SAVAGE WELLS
Sarah M. Eden

Biscuits with Raspberry Honey Butter

PREP AND COOKING TIME: 30 MIN · SERVES 10

BISCUITS

2 cups all-purpose flour	¼ teaspoon salt
2 teaspoons granulated sugar	½ cup butter
½ teaspoon cream of tartar	⅔ cup milk
1 tablespoon baking powder	

RASPBERRY HONEY BUTTER

1 cup butter, softened	½ cup raspberry preserves
½ cup honey	

1. **For the biscuits:** In a large mixing bowl, combine flour, sugar, cream of tartar, baking powder, and salt. Using a fork or your fingers, cut in butter until mixture resembles coarse crumbs. Make a well in the center of the bowl and add milk. Stir just until dough clings together. (A dough hook whisk on a stand mixer is best.)

2. On a lightly floured surface, knead dough gently for 10 to 12 strokes. Roll or pat dough to ½-inch thickness. Lightly dust a 2¼-inch round biscuit cutter with flour.

3. Making close cuts, press the biscuit cutter into the dough and drop the biscuit onto a large cookie sheet lined with parchment paper.

4. Bake at 425 degrees F. for 12 to 15 minutes or until tops begin to turn golden-brown.

5. **For the honey butter:** Place butter in a medium-size bowl and use a hand mixer to beat on medium-high for 5 minutes.

6. Add honey and raspberry preserves. Beat an additional 2 minutes, scraping down the sides of the bowl as needed. Serve with biscuits.

VARIATIONS

- Buttermilk biscuits: Prepare as above, except add ¼ teaspoon baking soda into flour mixture and substitute ¾ cup buttermilk for the milk.
- Drop biscuits: Prepare as above, except increase milk to 1 cup. Do not knead, roll, or cut dough. Drop dough by the spoonful onto the prepared cookie sheet. Makes 10 to 12 biscuits.
- For Thanksgiving and Christmas, substitute raspberry preserves with ½ cup homemade cranberry sauce.

NOTE

- Honey butter can be stored in the refrigerator for up to 1 week. Remove from refrigerator at least 30 minutes before serving.

He'd never looked at her so closely before, but the smoothness of her skin and perfect shape of her nose and chin impressed upon him just how beautiful she was.

PROMISES AND PRIMROSES
Josi S. Kilpack

Wyoming Timeline

1807 John Colter is the first White American known to enter present-day Wyoming

1834 Fort Laramie is the first permanent trading post established in Wyoming

1836 Narcissa Whitman and Eliza Spalding are the first White women to pass over the Oregon Trail

1847 Members of The Church of Jesus Christ of Latter-day Saints migrate through Wyoming to Utah

1860 Pony Express begins

1867 Union Pacific Railroad enters Wyoming

1868 Wyoming Territory created

1869 Wyoming women are given the right to vote

1872 Yellowstone Park is created

1883 Electric lights introduced in Cheyenne

1890 Wyoming Territory admitted into Union as the 44th state

NOTABLE NOVELS OF THE 19TH CENTURY

The Scarlet Letter by Nathaniel Hawthorne (1850)

Moby-Dick; or, The Whale by Herman Melville (1851)

Uncle Tom's Cabin by Harriet Beecher Stowe (1852)

Little Women by Louisa May Alcott (1868)

The Portrait of a Lady by Henry James (1881)

Adventures of Huckleberry Finn by Mark Twain (1884)

The Red Badge of Courage by Stephen Crane (1895)

Overnight Baked French Toast with Buttermilk Caramel Syrup

PREP AND COOKING TIME: 45 MIN
CHILL TIME: 8 HOURS (OR OVERNIGHT) · SERVES 12

FRENCH TOAST

½ cup butter

1 cup packed brown sugar

2 tablespoons light corn syrup

5 eggs

1½ cups half-and-half

½ teaspoon salt

1 teaspoon vanilla extract

1 teaspoon cinnamon (optional)

12 slices Texas toast, French bread, or challah bread

BUTTERMILK CARAMEL SYRUP

1 cup butter

1 cup granulated sugar

⅓ cup buttermilk

1 tablespoon light corn syrup

½ teaspoon baking soda

1 tablespoon vanilla extract

whipping cream, whipped (optional)

fresh fruit (optional)

vanilla ice cream (optional)

He leaned in close to her. He'd never known anyone whose eyes were as purely brown as hers. Not even a flake of any other color touched their depths. Beautiful. Simply beautiful.

HOPE SPRINGS
Sarah M. Eden

1. **For the French toast:** In a small saucepan, melt butter, brown sugar, and light corn syrup over medium heat until smooth. Pour mixture onto a greased 15x10x1 baking sheet (jelly roll pan). Spread mixture until smooth and even.

2. Place 12 slices of bread in a single layer to cover baking sheet.

3. In a medium-size bowl, mix together eggs, half-and-half, salt, vanilla, and cinnamon.

4. Spoon mixture over each slice of bread. Cover in foil and refrigerate overnight.

5. When ready to serve, bake covered French toast at 350 degrees F. for 15 minutes. Uncover, flip toast slices, and bake an additional 15 minutes.

6. Serve immediately with Buttermilk Caramel Syrup.

7. **For the syrup:** In a large saucepan, combine butter, sugar, buttermilk, light corn syrup, and baking soda. Bring to a boil and boil gently 5 minutes.

8. Remove from heat and stir in vanilla extract. Cool to room temperature.

9. Top French toast with syrup, whipping cream, fresh fruit, or a scoop of vanilla ice cream.

NOTES

- A metal baking sheet will produce a crispier French toast. A glass baking dish will make a softer French toast.
- If you are not serving the toast immediately after baking, turn bread over to prevent it from sticking to the bottom of the baking sheet.
- When making the syrup, make sure to use a large pan as the sauce typically expands.
- Syrup can be stored in the refrigerator for up to 1 week in an airtight container. Reheat prior to serving.

VARIATION

MIXED BERRY SAUCE

PREP AND COOKING TIME: 20 MIN · CHILL TIME: 1 HOUR
SERVES 8 TO 10

---

1 pound fresh strawberries, thinly sliced

6 ounces fresh blackberries

6 ounces fresh raspberries

1 tablespoon lemon juice

½ cup granulated sugar

1. Wash and drain berries. Combine berries in a large bowl and stir gently to combine. Place ⅓ of the mixed berries in a small bowl and refrigerate. Transfer the remaining berries into a medium saucepan.

2. Add lemon juice and sugar. Bring mixture to a gentle boil over medium heat. Cook 5 minutes or until berries turn into a syrup.

3. Transfer hot berries to a blender or use an immersion blender and purée until smooth. Set a fine mesh strainer over a bowl. Using a spoon or ladle, force the sauce through the strainer and into the bowl. Discard any remaining seeds. Refrigerate berry sauce until cold, about 1 hour.

4. When ready to serve, add the reserved berries to the sauce and stir to combine. If the sauce is too thick, add a few tablespoons of water, a little at a time, until the desired consistency is reached.

> **DID YOU KNOW?** The Acoma Pueblo in New Mexico has been inhabited since the twelfth century.

NOTE

- If using frozen berries, thaw and drain any excess liquid.

Rhubarb Coffee Cake

PREP AND COOKING TIME: 1 HOUR 20 MIN · SERVES 12 TO 15

CAKE

¼ teaspoon salt

1 teaspoon baking soda

2 cups all-purpose flour

½ cup butter, softened

1½ cups brown sugar

1 large egg

1 teaspoon vanilla extract

1 cup buttermilk or sour cream

2 cups rhubarb, washed and
chopped into ½-inch cubes

TOPPING

½ cup chopped pecans or walnuts

½ cup granulated sugar

1½ teaspoons ground cinnamon

1. **For the cake:** In a medium-size mixing bowl, sift together, salt, baking soda, and all-purpose flour.

2. Using either a stand mixer or a hand mixer with a large mixing bowl, cream butter and brown sugar together for 3 minutes or until light and fluffy. Add egg and vanilla extract. Mix well.

3. Mix in buttermilk and dry ingredients alternately. Add rhubarb and stir with spoon or rubber spatula until combined.

4. **For the topping:** In a small bowl, combine chopped nuts, granulated sugar, and cinnamon. Sprinkle topping onto cake and press slightly into cake with a hand or spatula.

5. Spray 9x13-inch baking dish with nonstick cooking spray. Pour cake mix into pan and bake at 350 degrees F. for 45 to 50 minutes or until cake tester comes out clean.

6. Serve warm with vanilla ice cream.

VARIATION

• Rhubarb Coffee Cake Muffins: Line 12 muffin tins and spoon mixture into cups until two-thirds full. Bake at 350 degrees F. for 20 to 25 minutes or until muffins pop up in the center.

NOTE

• Frozen rhubarb can be used in place of fresh rhubarb.

Their lips hovered not even a breath apart. It was a torturous, wonderful sort of agony. An uncertain promise. A fragile hope.

Then she—*she*—closed the minuscule distance. *She* kissed *him*.

HEALING HEARTS
Sarah M. Eden

BBQ Buffet

White Lightning Moonshine (Sweet Tea)

PREP TIME: 5 MIN · YIELDS 2 SERVINGS

2 herbal tea bags (mint, orange, chamomile)

4 cups filtered water, divided

4 to 8 ice cubes, depending on their size

1. In a teakettle, bring 1 cup of water to boil.
2. Place tea bags in a heat-resistant container.
3. Pour boiling water over tea bags and steep for 5 to 10 minutes. (The longer the steep time, the stronger the tea.)
4. In a pitcher, add ice cubes. Add remaining 3 cups cold water. Discard tea bags and add the steeped tea to the pitcher.
5. Chill and serve.

DID YOU KNOW? When tea was scarce, settlers on the frontier made drinks from sage, sassafras, and mint. Wild honey was used in place of sugar.

"The town is named after her moonshine."

Cade stopped on the spot, mouth agape. "Savage Wells is named after bootleg whiskey?"

Did he never listen to her? "She doesn't make whiskey."

THE SHERIFFS OF SAVAGE WELLS
Sarah M. Eden

NOTES
- For a fun presentation, serve sweet tea in a mason jar.
- Add diced fruit to ice cube tray before freezing for a refreshing zing of flavor.

Ten Tips for Setting Up a Buffet

1. Vary the height of the dishes by using raised platters.

2. Have a clear beginning so guests know where to pick up their plates.

3. Label and identify dishes. Include a list of important ingredients that might cause allergic reactions like shellfish or peanuts.

4. Group similar foods and flavors together. Save desserts for the end of the buffet or place on a separate table.

5. Keep the lines moving along both sides of the table by having more than one serving utensil available when possible.

6. Include smaller plates next to the food dishes where guests can place the serving utensils.

7. Place utensils at the end of the buffet so guests don't have to juggle silverware along with their plates.

8. Decorate the buffet table with tablecloths, garlands, streamers, twinkle lights, candles, or flowers.

9. Coordinate table linens and napkins with serving platters and dishes so your event theme is cohesive.

10. Provide plenty of trash cans to help keep the party environment clean.

Cowboy Caviar

PREP AND COOKING TIME: 20 MIN · SERVES 12

CAVIAR

1½ cups fresh or frozen sweet corn

1 (15-ounce) can black beans

1 (15-ounce) can black-eyed peas

3 Roma tomatoes, diced and seeds removed

⅓ cup red onion, finely chopped

1 bell pepper (red, yellow, or green), diced

¼ cup chopped cilantro

1 jalapeño pepper, seeds removed, finely diced (optional)

DRESSING

⅓ cup olive oil

2 tablespoons red wine vinegar

2 tablespoons lime juice, fresh

1 teaspoon granulated sugar

½ teaspoon salt

½ teaspoon black pepper

¼ teaspoon garlic powder

2 large avocados, pitted and diced

1. **For the caviar:** In a large bowl, combine corn, black beans, black-eyed peas, tomatoes, bell pepper, cilantro, and jalapeno pepper. Stir until ingredients are well combined.

2. **For the dressing:** In a separate bowl, whisk together olive oil, red wine vinegar, lime juice, sugar, salt, pepper, and garlic powder.

3. Pour dressing over caviar and mix well.

4. When ready to serve, add avocado. If not ready to serve, keep refrigerated, and be sure to stir well before serving.

VARIATIONS

- For a spicier salad, add ⅛ to ¼ teaspoon of chili powder and cumin to the dressing.
- Top with tortilla chips and serve alongside grilled steak, chicken, shrimp, or quinoa.

He had hair the color of a lake in the darkest hours of night, and a teasing hint of a smile played on his lips. He sat with one arm bent over the bench back, his sleeves rolled up, collar hanging limply open. Something his companion said brought out his smile. Where he'd been handsome before, the change rendered him rather breathtaking.

LONGING
FOR HOME
Sarah M. Eden

AMERICAN WEST: BBQ Buffet

NOTE

- This salad can be made ahead of time and kept refrigerated for up to 2 days. Stir well and add avocado before serving.

Smoky Beef and Bacon Chili

PREP AND COOKING TIME: 1 HOUR 15 MIN · SERVES 6 TO 8

2 slices thick-cut savory bacon, finely chopped

1 large onion, finely chopped

1 large clove garlic, minced

1 pound ground beef

1 tablespoon chili powder

1½ teaspoons cumin

1½ teaspoons smoked paprika

½ teaspoon cayenne pepper

1 teaspoon salt

¼ teaspoon pepper

1 (14-ounce) can diced tomatoes

1 (8-ounce) can tomato sauce

1 cup beef broth

1 teaspoon Worcestershire sauce

½ teaspoon smoke flavor (optional)

1 (15.5-ounce) can pinto beans, drained and rinsed

1 (15.5-ounce) can black beans, drained and rinsed

1 (15.5-ounce) can kidney beans, drained and rinsed

Sour cream, shredded sharp cheddar cheese, and green onions for garnish

1. In a heavy stockpot, cook bacon over medium heat until it begins to brown.

2. Add onion and garlic and reduce heat to low. Cook until onion is translucent.

3. Increase heat to medium and add ground beef. Stir until ground beef is brown.

4. Add chili powder, cumin, paprika, cayenne pepper, salt, and pepper and stir until well mixed.

5. Add tomatoes, tomato sauce, beef broth, Worcestershire sauce, and smoke flavor. Increase heat to high and bring to a boil.

6. Partially cover stockpot with lid, then reduce heat and simmer 30 minutes to 1 hour.

7. Uncover pot. Add beans and stir. Cook uncovered 10 minutes.

8. Serve with sour cream, cheese and onions.

NOTE

· This chili can be made ahead of time and stored in an airtight container in the refrigerator for up to 3 days. The longer the chili sits, the more flavorful it becomes.

He was handsome, Anna thought again, with his hand shielding his face and his foot perched on a coil of rope, his expression serious. She was rather shaken that he had such an effect on her senses, and that she couldn't stop gazing at him.

LADY ANNA'S FAVOR
Karen Tuft

Golden Cornbread with Honey Butter

PREP AND COOKING TIME: 35 MIN · SERVES 6 TO 8

CORNBREAD

½ cup coarse cornmeal

½ cup flour

1 teaspoon salt

3 teaspoons baking powder

¼ teaspoon sugar

1 cup buttermilk

1 large egg

2 tablespoons mayonnaise (optional)

1 cup cooked corn (optional)

2 to 3 tablespoons cooking oil or bacon grease

HONEY BUTTER

1 tablespoon honey

½ cup butter, room temperature

1. **For cornbread:** In a large bowl, mix together cornmeal, flour, salt, baking powder, and sugar.

2. Mix in buttermilk until just incorporated. Add egg and mix again. Add mayonnaise and mix again. Don't overmix.

3. Add corn, if desired.

4. Add cooking oil to an oven-safe cast-iron skillet and place in a 425 degree F. oven for 5 to 6 minutes until oil is sizzling hot.

5. Pull out skillet, add dough. Dough should sizzle.

6. Return skillet to the oven and bake for 25 to 30 minutes, or until the top is golden brown.

7. **For honey butter:** In a small bowl, blend honey with butter using a hand mixer until smooth.

8. Serve cornbread hot with butter.

One moment he was looking down at her with those eyes, and in the next, he cradled her face in his hands and kissed her.

THE VICAR'S DAUGHTER
Josi S. Kilpack

AMERICAN WEST: BBQ Buffet

Tasty Barbeque Bites

PREP AND COOKING TIME: 1 HOUR · SERVES 8

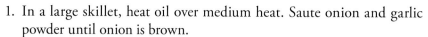

1 tablespoon olive oil

½ cup chopped onion

½ teaspoon garlic powder

1 pound shredded pork or chicken

1½ cups BBQ sauce

1 (10-ounce) package refrigerated biscuits

2 cups shredded sharp cheddar

1. In a large skillet, heat oil over medium heat. Saute onion and garlic powder until onion is brown.

2. Add shredded pork and BBQ sauce. Saute 5 minutes or until pork is heated through.

3. On a floured surface, roll out each biscuit. Line cups and sides of a large, lightly greased muffin tin or individual ramekins with flattened biscuit.

4. Fill each biscuit to the top with meat-and-onion mixture.

5. Top each cup with cheddar cheese.

6. Bake at 400 degrees F. for 20 minutes or until cheese has melted and the tops are golden brown. Bake up to an additional 5 minutes if needed.

7. Remove from oven and allow to cool for 2 to 3 minutes. Biscuits should remove easily from the tin with a spoon. If using ramekins, serve directly from the oven.

VARIATIONS

- BBQ Poppers: Wrap the BBQ pork mixture and cheese inside a biscuit. Seal the dough and place in lightly greased small muffin tin. Bake at 400 degrees F. for 20 minutes.

Oh, that was a coquettish look if he'd ever seen one. This woman was trouble, the kind he rather enjoyed sorting out.

WYOMING WILD
Sarah M. Eden

DID YOU KNOW? The first dime novels were published right before the American Civil War. Filled with adventure and romance, these stories gave those in the North a colorful if not jaded view of the Wild West.

AMERICAN WEST: BBQ Buffet

He Loves Me, He Loves Me Not

CURIOUS IF HE LIKES YOU? Here are some fun courtship customs from the American West that you can use to determine if it's true love.

- Peel an apple into a single curl and toss the skin over your shoulder. The apple peel will fall into the shape of your true love's initials.

- Gaze into the tea leaves at the bottom of the cup to gain clues into who your true love might be.

- "Pull the kale" by uprooting cabbages and reading the shape of the root to learn the name of the boy who likes you.

- Shake a new quilt out the door and the first man who enters the door will be your future husband.

- Gaze over your shoulder into a mirror to catch a glimpse of your true love's reflection.

- Throw a newly finished quilt at the first single man you see to charm him into courtship.

Savage Wells is my home, and I cain't imagine it without you here."

"Neither can I," she said. "John Hawking, you are home to me."

She hooked her arms around his neck, just as he set his around her once more.

"I love you," she said.

"And I love you more than I thought I could. You taught me that love ain't weakness."

"Promise that after you finish each new marshaling trip, you'll always come back here, back home to me?"

"Always," he whispered in the breath before he kissed her once more. This time, it was the fervent heart-pounding kiss of a man who'd found love and a woman who meant to claim it.

WYOMING WILD
Sarah M. Eden

Gooseberry Pie

PREP AND COOKING TIME: 1 HOUR 20 MIN · CHILL TIME: 1 HOUR
SERVES 8

CRUST

1½ cup all-purpose flour

½ teaspoon salt

4 ounces lard

5 to 7 tablespoons cold water

FILLING

1 (15-ounce) can gooseberries, drain
and reserve juice

½ cup water

¾ cup granulated sugar

¼ cup all-purpose flour

⅛ teaspoon salt

2 tablespoons of butter, or 4 dabs

1. **For the crust:** In a small bowl, mix flour and salt, add lard and cut into mixture until crumbly. Gradually add cold water, tossing with a fork until dough holds together when pressed.

2. Shape dough into a disc. Wrap in plastic wrap and refrigerate at least 1 hour or overnight.

3. On a lightly floured surface, divide dough and roll each half into a ⅛-inch-thick circle. Transfer one crust to the bottom of a 9-inch pie pan. Trim crust to ½-inch past the rim of the pie pan.

4. **For the filling:** In a medium-size saucepan, add the reserved juice from the canned gooseberries and water. Bring to a boil.

5. In a separate bowl, mix sugar, flour, and salt. Add to boiling mixture and cook on medium heat for 8 to 12 minutes until thickened.

6. Add drained gooseberries.

7. Pour gooseberry filling into uncooked pie shell.

8. Add 4 dabs of butter to the top of the filling.

9. Cover with the other uncooked pie crust. Flute or crimp crust and add four slits near the center of the top pie crust.

10. Bake at 400 degrees F. for 10 minutes. Remove from oven and cover pie crust edges with aluminum foil. Reduce heat to 350 degrees F. and bake 40 to 45 minutes until crust is golden brown.

11. Remove pie from oven and allow to cool on a wire rack for 20 minutes before serving.

NOTES

- You can substitute the lard with chilled butter.
- To save time, use a store-bought crust or your own favorite pie crust recipe.
- Fruit pies are best stored at room temperature and eaten within 2 days. They can also be refrigerated for up to 5 days.

Mr. Ellis. Nora had tried to put him out of her mind since the moment she'd left the stables the other day. He was far too handsome for his own good. And for her own good.

WINDSONG
MANOR
Julie Wright

Peach Cobbler

PREP AND COOKING TIME: 1 HOUR · SERVES 8

PEACHES

4 cups peaches (about 5 peaches), peeled, pitted, and sliced

¼ teaspoon salt

¾ cup granulated sugar

6 tablespoons butter

BATTER

1 cup granulated sugar

1 cup all-purpose flour

¼ teaspoon salt

2 teaspoons baking powder

¾ cup milk

ground cinnamon

1. **For the peaches:** In a saucepan, add sliced peaches, salt, and granulated sugar. Cook on medium heat until sugar is dissolved and the juice from the peaches has been released. Remove from heat and set aside.

2. Slice butter into pieces and add to a 9x13-inch baking dish. Place pan in a warm oven, allowing the butter to melt. Once melted, remove pan from the oven. Set aside.

3. **For the batter:** In a large bowl, whisk together sugar, flour, salt, and baking powder. Whisk in milk and stir until just combined. Pour mixture into buttered pan and smooth into an even layer.

4. **To assemble the cobbler:** Spoon peaches and juice over the batter. Sprinkle ground cinnamon generously over the top.

5. Bake at 350 degrees F. for 40 to 45 minutes or until top is golden brown.

6. Serve warm with a scoop of vanilla ice cream or topped with whipped cream.

The other dancers had already begun their twirling trip around the room. Gideon slipped an arm around Miriam's waist and swung them out amongst the others.

HEALING HEARTS
Sarah M. Eden

NOTES

- Instead of fresh peaches, use bottled or canned peaches. If using canned peaches, don't drain liquid, then add ⅛ cup sugar and 2 tablespoons lemon juice.
- This can also be baked for 35 minutes in a Dutch oven.

CELEBRATIONS

CELEBRATIONS are the poetry of life, where joy dances and hearts connect in the most enchanting ways. They transcend time and space, bringing souls together to honor love, tradition, and the magic of togetherness. Whether it's the passionate embrace shared on Valentine's Day, a weekend road trip with friends, a fall evening cozied up before a fireplace, or the gentle warmth of Christmas filled with laughter and nostalgia, each celebration is a tapestry of emotions—laughter, memories, and dreams.

Valentine's Day

Infused Water

PREP TIME: 5 MIN · CHILL TIME: 1 HOUR (OR OVERNIGHT)
SERVES APPROXIMATELY 6 PEOPLE

12 cups chilled water (can be still or sparkling)

2 large lemons, sliced thinly

1 large cucumber, sliced

12 mint leaves

1. Pour water into a large pitcher.

2. Add lemon and cucumber slices.

3. Rub mint leaves in your hand until they become fragrant to release the mint oils.

4. Add mint leaves to the water.

5. Chill at least 1 hour before serving. Can chill overnight.

VARIATIONS

• Pineapple-orange: 1 large orange, sliced, and 1 cup fresh pineapple chunks
• Lemon-lime: 1 large lemon, sliced, and 2 limes, sliced
• Herbal: Basil, rosemary, or lavender (rinse before using)
• Berry: 1 cup sliced strawberries, and 1 cup of other berries
• Watermelon: 2 cups cubed watermelon

This time I knew enough to kiss him back. He caught his breath, and then I felt his lips curl up into his wicked grin. It was delicious.

EDENBROOKE
Julianne Donaldson

NOTE
• Feel free to use other fruit and herb combinations for a fun and refreshing infused water.

Afternoon Drinking Chocolate

PREP AND COOKING TIME: 10 MIN · SERVES 4

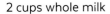

2 cups whole milk

8 ounces semisweet chocolate, chopped

pinch of salt

2 teaspoons vanilla extract

1. In a small, heavy-bottomed saucepan, combine milk, chocolate, and salt.
2. Heat gently over low heat, whisking regularly, until chocolate is completely melted. Don't let it come to a simmer.
3. Once chocolate is melted and combined, stir in vanilla.
4. Pour into small, individual mugs and top with whipped cream and additional chocolate shavings if you like.

VARIATIONS

- Add a pinch of ground cinnamon along with the salt.
- Instead of plain semisweet chocolate, use peppermint baking chips.
- Drizzle salted caramel on top of the whipping cream.
- Add 1 teaspoon Irish cream syrup or other flavored syrups in step 1.

Mrs. Latham picked up the pot to pour, a rich stream of drinking chocolate spilling from its short spout and filling each white cup.

GAMES IN A BALLROOM
Jentry Flint

> DID YOU KNOW? Valentine's Day is commonly associated with Saint Valentine, a Christian martyr who lived during the third century. There are several legends about Saint Valentine, but one popular story suggests he was a priest who performed secret weddings for soldiers who were forbidden to marry.

NOTE

- Cooking the hot chocolate slowly over a low heat helps the chocolate to melt completely instead of remaining speckled.

The Language of Flowers

IN THE VICTORIAN ERA, flowers were a language all their own. From the type of blossom chosen to the way the ribbon was tied on a bouquet to even which hand gave or received the flowers all carried meaning.

Calla Lily
beauty

Carnation
fascination

Daffodil
unequaled love

Daisy
innocence

Gardenia
secret love

Hyacinth
playful

Iris
hope

Peony
bashful

Poppy
consolation

Red rose
love

Sweet William
gallantry

Tiger Lily
wealth

Fondues

CHOCOLATE FONDUE

PREP AND COOKING TIME: 15 MIN · SERVES 8 TO 12

DIPPERS

angel food cake or pound cake, cut into 1-inch cubes

apple slices

banana chunks

brownie bites

churros

cinnamon bears

cream puffs

donut holes

marshmallows

pineapple chunks

pretzels

rice cereal treats

strawberries

FONDUE

4 ounces milk chocolate, chopped

6 ounces semisweet chocolate, chopped

½ cup whipping cream

1½ tablespoons butter

½ teaspoon vanilla extract

⅛ teaspoon salt

1. Prepare desired dippers and arrange on a serving platter.

2. **For the fondue:** In a small microwave-safe bowl, combine the chocolates, whipping cream, and butter. Microwave in 30-second intervals, stirring after each interval, until smooth. If chocolate is too thick, add more whipping cream.

3. Stir in vanilla and salt.

4. Transfer to a fondue pot or small slow cooker to keep warm. Serve with dippers.

NOTE

· If fondue gets too thick, reheat in the microwave for 15 seconds until melted and smooth again.

CONTINUED ON NEXT PAGE

She smiled, a beautiful wide smile he remembered from their first meeting, from when he'd pulled back from their kiss and known that not only had she wanted him to kiss her but that she had been glad he did.

THE VALET'S SECRET
Josi S. Kilpack

CARAMEL FONDUE

PREP AND COOKING TIME: 15 MIN · SERVES 8 TO 12

DIPPERS

angel food cake or pound cake, cut into 1-inch cubes

apple slices

banana chunks

brownie bites

churros

cinnamon bears

cream puffs

donut holes

marshmallows

pineapple chunks

pretzels

rice cereal treats

strawberries

FONDUE

1 cup heavy whipping cream, divided

¾ cup granulated sugar

½ cup light corn syrup

¼ teaspoon salt

¼ cup butter

½ teaspoon vanilla extract

1. Prepare desired dippers and arrange on a serving platter.
2. **For the fondue:** In a heavy saucepan, combine ½ cup whipping cream, granulated sugar, corn syrup, and salt. Bring to a boil over medium heat until a candy thermometer reads 234 degrees F., or soft-ball stage, stirring constantly. Cool to 220 degrees F.
3. Stir in remaining whipping cream. Return to a boil.
4. Remove from heat and stir in vanilla extract.
5. Transfer to a fondue pot or small slow cooker to keep warm. Serve with dippers.

CHEESE FONDUE

PREP AND COOKING TIME: 15 MIN · SERVES 8 TO 12

DIPPERS

apple slices

carrot slices

cauliflower florets

meatballs, cooked

pretzels

rustic bread, cut into 1-inch cubes

steamed broccoli florets

FONDUE

1½ cups Swiss cheese, grated

2 cups Gruyère cheese, grated

2 tablespoons cornstarch

1 cup low-sodium chicken broth

⅛ teaspoon lemon juice

¼ teaspoon pepper

¼ teaspoon ground nutmeg

1 dash of paprika

1. Prepare desired dippers and arrange on a serving platter.

2. **For the fondue:** Place shredded cheeses in a gallon-size zip-top bag. Add cornstarch and shake until evenly coated.

3. In a medium-size saucepan, add chicken broth and lemon juice and bring to a simmer. Reduce heat to medium-low.

4. Add the cheeses, a small handful at a time, stirring constantly with a wooden spoon. Make sure to scrape the bottom of the pan to prevent scorching.

5. Once cheese is melted and begins to simmer, add the pepper, nutmeg, and paprika. If needed, add more cheese until desired consistency is reached.

6. Transfer to a fondue pot or small slow cooker to keep warm. Serve with dippers.

PIZZA FONDUE

PREP AND COOKING TIME: 15 MIN · SERVES 8 TO 12

DIPPERS

bell peppers, sliced	meatballs, cooked
bread, cut into 1-inch cubes	mozzarella cheese cubes
breadsticks, cut into 1-inch cubes	mushrooms
carrot slices	pepperoni, cut into 1-inch cubes
crackers	steamed broccoli florets

FONDUE

1 (24-ounce) jar marinara sauce	⅓ cup grated Parmesan cheese
2 cups mozzarella, shredded	¼ teaspoon dried oregano

1. Prepare desired dippers and arrange on a serving platter.

2. **For the fondue:** In a medium-size saucepan, add marinara sauce, mozzarella and Parmesan cheeses, and oregano.

3. Heat on medium for 5 to 10 minutes or until mozzarella cheese melts. Stir to combine.

4. Transfer to a fondue pot or small slow cooker to keep warm. Serve with dippers.

He touched Charlotte's bare arm just above her elbow, where her glove ended, and felt her startle. But she did not withdraw or give him a warning look. Instead she shifted toward him . . .

Walter took her movement as encouragement and curled his fingers under the fabric of her glove, the skin underneath as soft and smooth as the satin above. He paused, and when she did not protest, he began to slowly roll down her glove. First he revealed her elbow, then her forearm and finally her graceful wrist, pausing a moment to run his fingers from wrist to elbow and causing her to shiver slightly. He then pulled at the thumb of her glove, and she shifted again, her body turned toward him even more while her eyes stayed on the entertainment. Walter used his other hand to help him remove the glove one finger at a time, her breath becoming more shallow and the air between them increasing in warmth—the same warmth he felt within.

When their eyes met in the dim room, Walter's breath caught. She was lovely in the dim light, her golden gown sparkling like her eyes. Once her hand was bare, he fit his warm palm against hers, and wove his fingers into hers—watching her eyes the whole time.

She swallowed and her lips parted—filling him with such longing to kiss her that it was only a lifetime of good manners that kept him from doing so in this public place.

THE LADY OF THE LAKES
Josi S. Kilpack

Three-of-a-Kind Sherbet

PREP AND COOKING TIME: 1 HOUR 30 MIN
CHILL TIME: 4 HOURS (OR OVERNIGHT) · SERVES 12

3 cups granulated sugar

3 large, ripe bananas, mashed

1 cup freshly squeezed orange juice
(about 4 large oranges)

½ cup freshly squeezed lemon juice
(about 2 large lemons)

1 (6-ounce) can pineapple juice

1 (8-ounce) can crushed pineapple,
undrained

4 cups whole milk

2 cups half-and-half

2 cups whipping cream, whipped

1. In a large mixing bowl, combine sugar, bananas, orange juice, lemon juice, pineapple juice, and crushed pineapple. Mix until sugar is dissolved. Cover with plastic wrap and chill in the refrigerator.

2. Add milk, half-and-half, and whipping cream. Mix well.

3. Add mixture to an ice cream maker and freeze according to ice cream maker instructions.

4. Serve immediately, or transfer sherbet to an airtight, freezer-safe container and keep frozen until ready to serve. Allow sherbet to soften for 15 to 20 minutes at room temperature before serving.

We discussed favorite movies. . . . We debated between ice cream versus frozen yogurt, donuts versus brownies, and sleeping in versus watching sunrises.

LIES JANE
AUSTEN TOLD ME
Julie Wright

DID YOU KNOW? Chocolate in the seventeenth century was typically mixed with spices such as cinnamon and chili, sweetened with sugar, and sometimes thickened with eggs.

Chocolate-Dipped Strawberries

PREP AND COOKING TIME: 30 MIN · SERVES APPROXIMATELY 24

12 large strawberries, with stems

2 cups semisweet chocolate chips

1 to 2 tablespoons butter-flavored coconut oil

1. Rinse strawberries, leaving stems on. Blot dry with paper towels.

2. Line a standard cookie sheet with parchment paper.

3. In a medium-size microwave-safe dish, melt chocolate chips and coconut oil in 30-second intervals, stirring between each interval until smooth.

4. Dip each strawberry into chocolate and place on parchment paper.

5. Refrigerate 10 to 15 minutes or until chocolate is set. Gently loosen strawberries from parchment paper and serve.

VARIATIONS

- Dip strawberries in milk chocolate and drizzle with melted white chocolate, or dip in white chocolate and drizzle with milk chocolate.
- Dip strawberries in chocolate, then cover with sprinkles before placing in refrigerator.

"I want you to kiss me," she said, half-shocked, half-spurred by her own brevity. "Kiss me now or I'll lose my mind."

HEARTS OF BRIARWALL
Krista Jensen

CELEBRATIONS: Valentine's Day

NOTE
- Chocolate-covered strawberries can be stored in the refrigerator for up to 1 day.

Weekend Road Trip

Charcuterie Boards

Cured meats (prosciutto, ham, salami)

Cheeses (Havarti, Swiss, Brie, smoked Gouda, mozzarella)

Mixed olives

Honey

Dark chocolate

Pickles, sweet and dill

Mustard

Vegetables (broccoli, carrots, cucumbers, cauliflower, grape tomatoes, jicama, mini peppers, etc.)

Dips (see pages 8, 10)

Crackers and bread

Fig jam/spread

Nuts (pistachios, almonds, walnuts)

Dried fruits (apples, apricots, dates)

Fresh fruits (grapes, apples, berries)

1. Mix-and-match your favorite flavors and textures. Arrange items on a charcuterie board, large cutting board, or serving platter.

VARIATIONS:
- For a road-trip board, arrange your favorite travel dish with lid.
- For a party appetizer board, theme your boards: a fruit board, a cracker board, or a vegetable board with dips.
- For a large Christmas board, arrange your bites in the shape of a Christmas tree.

"On to our picnic! What shall we have? Fruits, cheeses, . . . salted ham?" Charlie's steps seemed springier than usual, and I felt a sudden urge to keep *his* pace instead of Liza's.

MISS NEWBURY'S LIST
Megan Walker

Watermelon Feta Salad

PREP AND COOKING TIME: 15 MIN · SERVES 10 TO 12

SALAD

8 cups watermelon, cubed

2 cups blueberries

6 ounces crumbled feta

1 cup pecans, chopped and toasted

1 (1.75-ounce) container microgreens

DRESSING

2 tablespoons cara cara vanilla balsamic vinegar

1 to 2 tablespoons orange olive oil

ALTERNATE DRESSING

2 tablespoons honey

2 tablespoons lime or orange juice

1 to 2 tablespoons extra-virgin olive oil

pinch of salt

1. In a large bowl, combine watermelon, blueberries, feta, toasted pecans, and microgreens.

2. Add balsamic and olive oil. Gently toss and serve immediately.

3. If you do not have infused olive oils and vinegars, whisk together honey, juice, olive oil, and a pinch of salt into a small bowl.

VARIATIONS

- Add cucumber, fresh peaches, avocado, jicama, strawberries, or pomegranate seeds.
- Substitute another cheese for feta.
- Use different infused olive oils and balsamic vinegars depending on what fruit is in season.
- Serve salad alongside any protein.

She fell against his chest, and he wrapped his hand around her waist, holding her against him, which ignited all the same feelings the dance had built between them. Her breath caught in her throat. For a moment, she thought he would kiss her.

DAISIES AND DEVOTION
Josi S. Kilpack

DID YOU KNOW? The Ladies' Automobile Association was founded in 1903 and twenty-three of the first fifty members were titled ladies of society.

Grandma's Snickerdoodles

PREP AND COOKING TIME: 30 MIN · MAKES 2 DOZEN COOKIES

COOKIES

1 cup butter, softened

1½ cups granulated sugar

2 eggs

2 teaspoons cream of tartar

½ teaspoon salt

2¾ cups all-purpose flour

1 teaspoon baking soda

TOPPING

2 tablespoons granulated sugar

1 teaspoon ground cinnamon

1. **For the cookies:** In a stand mixer or using a hand mixer, cream butter, granulated sugar, and eggs for 2 minutes or until light and fluffy.

2. In a separate small bowl, sift together cream of tartar, salt, flour, and baking soda.

3. Add to creamed mixture and mix until combined.

4. **For the topping:** In a small bowl, combine granulated sugar and cinnamon.

5. Using a medium-size cookie scoop, make the cookies into balls and roll dough balls in the cinnamon-sugar topping.

6. Place 12 balls on a cookie sheet lined with parchment paper. Bake at 375 degrees F. for 8 to 10 minutes.

7. Allow cookies to cool on baking sheet for 10 minutes, then transfer to a wire rack to cool completely.

DID YOU KNOW? In 1902, the speed limit for automobiles was twelve miles per hour.

Over the last two years, I'd tried so hard not to imagine life outside of the safety of Winterset, but as we stood so close together in the library, moonlight sparkling in Oliver's eyes, I dared to dream.

WINTERSET
Tiffany Odekirk

Road Trip Playlist

1. "A Thousand Miles" by Vanessa Carlton
2. "Proud Mary" by Tina Turner
3. "Go Your Own Way" by Fleetwood Mac
4. "Livin' on a Prayer" by Bon Jovi
5. "Runnin' Down a Dream" by Tom Petty
6. "Every Day Is a Winding Road" by Sheryl Crow
7. "Sweet Home Alabama" by Lynyrd Skynyrd
8. "Life Is a Highway" by Rascal Flatts
9. "Take Me Home, Country Roads" by John Denver
10. "Sweet Caroline" by Neil Diamond
11. "Fast Car" by Tracy Chapman
12. "I'm Gonna Be (500 Miles)" by The Proclaimers
13. "Ramble On" by Led Zeppelin
14. "Toto" by Africa
15. "Walking in Memphis" by Marc Cohen
16. "Walking on Sunshine" by Katrina and the Waves
17. "Total Eclipse of the Heart" by Bonnie Tyler
18. "I Will Always Love You" by Whitney Houston
19. "Don't Stop Believin'" by Journey

Chocolate Mint Brownies

PREP AND COOKING TIME: 45 MIN
MAKES 12 LARGE OR 24 SMALL BROWNIES

BROWNIES

1 cup butter, melted

1 cup cocoa powder

2 cups granulated sugar

4 large eggs

1¼ cups all-purpose flour

½ teaspoon salt

1 (10-ounce) bag crème de menthe (mint) baking chips, divided

TOPPING

12 ounces semisweet chocolate chips

⅓ cup milk

1. **For the brownies:** In a large mixing bowl, whisk melted butter and cocoa powder until combined.

2. Add sugar and mix well.

3. Stir in eggs one at a time.

4. Add flour and salt, stirring until well combined.

5. Stir in half of the bag of mint baking chips.

6. Spread the prepared brownie mix into a 9x13-inch baking pan sprayed with nonstick cooking spray and bake at 350 degrees F. for 20 minutes or until a toothpick inserted into the center comes out clean or with only a few fudgy crumbs.

7. Cool brownies on a wire rack.

8. **For the topping:** Add chocolate to a small glass bowl and set aside. In a small saucepan, heat milk just until it starts to simmer, about 1 minute. Pour over chocolate and stir until smooth.

9. Pour chocolate over cooled brownies and sprinkle with remaining baking chips.

VARIATIONS

• Toffee Bit Brownies: Instead of mint baking chips, use 1 bag of baking toffee bits or about 1½ cups chopped toffee candy bars. Add 1 cup of the bits to the brownie mixture in step 5 and sprinkle the rest over the chocolate topping.

• Peanut Butter Fudge Brownies: Omit the mint baking chips for the brownies and top with recipe on page 160.

CONTINUED ON NEXT PAGE

No one . . . could mistake her for anything but a beautiful woman coming into her own.

Everything about her reminded him of a summer stroll in a midnight garden.

HEARTS OF BRIARWALL
Krista Jensen

CELEBRATIONS: Weekend Road Trip

TOPPING FOR PEANUT BUTTER FUDGE BROWNIES

2 cups creamy peanut butter

½ cup butter, chopped into pieces

1 teaspoon vanilla extract

2¼ cups powdered sugar

1 tablespoon milk, if needed

1. In a large microwave-safe glass bowl, combine peanut butter and butter. Microwave in 20-second intervals until butter is melted and mixture is smooth.

2. Mix in vanilla extract.

3. Gradually stir in powdered sugar until combined. If mixture is too thick, add milk.

4. Drop by cookie scoops or spoonfuls over cooled brownies.

5. Using a knife, gently spread the mixture over the brownies. Then add the chocolate topping.

DID YOU KNOW? The first all-British four-wheel car was designed and built by Herbert Austin in 1900.

Orange Chocolate Chip Cookies

PREP AND COOKING TIME: 1 HOUR · MAKES 4 DOZEN COOKIES

3¼ cups all-purpose flour

1 teaspoon salt

½ teaspoon baking soda

2 teaspoons cornstarch

1 teaspoon baking powder

1 cup firmly packed light brown sugar

1 cup granulated sugar

1 cup butter, softened

2 large eggs

1 teaspoon vanilla extract

1 tablespoon orange zest (about 1 large orange)

1 teaspoon orange extract

1 cup semisweet chocolate chips

1 cup milk chocolate chips

1. In a large bowl, whisk together flour, salt, baking soda, cornstarch, and baking powder. Set aside.

2. Using a stand mixer, cream together brown sugar, granulated sugar, and butter 3 to 4 minutes or until light and fluffy. Add in 1 egg at a time, incorporating fully after each one.

3. Mix in vanilla, orange zest, and orange extract.

4. Slowly add in flour mixture and mix until incorporated. Using a heavy spatula, gently stir in chocolate chips.

5. Using a cookie scoop, drop dough onto a cookie sheet that has been lined with parchment paper or sprayed with a nonstick cooking spray.

6. Bake at 350 degrees F. for 9 to 11 minutes.

7. Allow cookies to cool on a cookie sheet for 2 minutes before transferring to a wire rack to cool completely.

VARIATION

• This recipe works well with any combination of chocolate chips. Use white chocolate chips instead of semisweet chocolate chips.

Their lips touched with a jolt . . . A wave of heat poured through [Amie], awakening all her senses. She leaned into it, letting the feeling consume her. Somewhere, a voice screamed for her to stop, while another insisted she make the kiss look as real as possible. The third voice was the loudest and the strongest, and it declared kissing to be the most wonderful experience of her life.

THE RULES OF MATRIMONY
Anneka R. Walker

CELEBRATIONS: Weekend Road Trip

Hawaiian Luau

Hawaiian Beverages

TROPICAL PIÑA COLADA

PREP TIME: 5 MIN · SERVES 8

2 cups real cream of coconut

2 cups pineapple juice

8 cups ice

fresh pineapple wedges

1. In a blender, combine all ingredients and mix well.
2. Pour into individual glasses and garnish with a fresh pineapple wedge.

NOTE
· May have to make multiple batches.

LUAU PUNCH

PREP TIME: 5 MIN · YIELDS 30 1-CUP SERVINGS

1½ cups frozen orange juice concentrate

6 cups 100% pineapple juice, divided

2 liters lemon-lime soda

1. In a large pitcher, mix orange juice concentrate with 3 cups pineapple juice until combined. Add the remaining pineapple juice and lemon-lime soda.
2. Serve in a large punch bowl or in individual glasses over ice.

MAI TAI MOCKTAIL

PREP TIME: 5 MIN · SERVES 8

3 cups orange juice

1 cup lime juice

½ cup orgeat syrup (almond syrup)

½ cup grenadine

8 teaspoons fine sugar

8 cups ice

fresh lime slices

maraschino cherries

1. In a large pitcher, combine orange juice, lime juice, orgeat syrup, grenadine, and sugar. Mix until sugar is dissolved.
2. When ready to serve, pour over ice and garnish with a fresh lime slice and a maraschino cherry.

I've seen thousands of sunrises in my lifetime, and they've all been beautiful. Hawaiian sunrises are my favorite, so I didn't mind waking early to witness one this morning. Its beauty was unrivaled.

A SONG FOR THE STARS
Ilima Todd

Ono Salad

PREP AND COOKING TIME: 20 MIN · SERVES 8

DRESSING

3 tablespoons tahini sauce

4 teaspoons maple syrup or honey

2 tablespoons apple cider vinegar

2 tablespoons pineapple juice

salt and pepper to taste

SALAD

4 cups baby spinach or baby lettuce

4 cups purple cabbage, finely chopped

2 cups chopped papaya or mango

2 cups chopped pineapple

1½ cups roasted macadamia nuts

fresh black pepper

½ cup coconut flakes (optional)

1. **For the dressing:** Whisk together tahini sauce, maple syrup, apple cider vinegar, and pineapple juice. Add salt and pepper to taste. Set aside.

2. **For the salad:** In a large bowl, add spinach or lettuce. Add chopped cabbage. Gently toss greens with 2 to 4 tablespoons of dressing.

3. Add chopped fruit and nuts to salad.

4. Drizzle remaining dressing on top.

5. Serve family-style or portioned into individual bowls.

This is what I wanted. To feel connected to him. To know that no matter where either of us is in the world, we are linked. By nature, by our memories. By the traditions we've shared with each other.

A SONG FOR THE STARS
Ilima Todd

DID YOU KNOW? In eighteenth century Hawaii, the men did all the cooking, and the men and women ate separately.

NOTE
• Chicken, ahi tuna, pork, or shrimp pair well with this salad.

Peppered Pork Tenderloin

PREP AND COOKING TIME: 60 MIN · SERVES 6 TO 8

1 teaspoon cinnamon

1 teaspoon chili powder

1 teaspoon ground cumin

2 teaspoons salt

½ teaspoon black pepper

2 pork tenderloins (2- to 2½-pounds total)

2 tablespoons extra-virgin olive oil

1 cup packed brown sugar (light or dark brown)

2 tablespoons finely chopped garlic

1 tablespoon hot sauce (use less for a more mild flavor)

1. In a small bowl, mix cinnamon, chili powder, cumin, salt, and pepper. Rub mixture over tenderloin by hand.

2. Add olive oil to an oven-safe skillet over medium-high heat until oil is hot.

3. Place tenderloin in skillet and allow to brown for 3 to 4 minutes, turning the meat to sear all sides.

4. In a separate bowl, mix together brown sugar, garlic, and hot sauce. Spread mixture over meat.

5. Transfer skillet to oven and bake at 350 degrees F. for 20 to 25 minutes or until pork reaches 140 degrees F. on a meat thermometer. Allow pork to rest 10 minutes at room temperature. (Temperature will likely rise to 155 degrees F.)

6. Cut meat into 1- to 2-inch-thick slices and serve with leftover glaze.

7. Strain the pork drippings from the pan through a sieve and then serve over the pork.

VARIATION

- Use chicken breasts instead of pork tenderloin. Bake at 350 degrees F. for 25 to 30 minutes.

Lit torches surround the clearing. A tangy scent of flowers mixed with salt pork hangs in the air. A cloud of smoke rises from the south end where firepits recently held cooked meats and vegetables.

A SONG FOR THE STARS
Ilima Todd

NOTES

- If you don't have an oven-safe skillet, sear the tenderloin in a regular skillet, then transfer meat to a greased, rimmed baking pan or casserole dish for the baking portion.

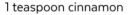

CELEBRATIONS: Hawaiian Luau

Hawaiian Game

KŌNANE: AN ANCIENT HAWAIIAN GAME OF STRATEGY
2 players

GAME SETUP: The game is played on a rectangular board with an even number of rows and columns. The most common size is 8x8 —the same size as a checkerboard—but other sizes can also be used. Completely fill the board with black and white stones arranged in an alternating pattern. The starting player removes one of their own pieces from either the center of the board or one of the four corners. The opponent then removes an adjacent piece of their own color. This creates the initial empty spaces on the board.

HOW TO PLAY:
• Moves: Players take turns making moves, which consist of jumping one of your pieces over an adjacent opponent's piece, landing in an empty space directly beyond it. The jumped piece is then captured and removed from the board.
• Jumping: Players can only jump horizontally or vertically, not diagonally. Multiple jumps are allowed in a single turn, however, as long as each jump lands in an empty space.

WINNING THE GAME: The game continues until one player can no longer make a legal move. That player loses the game, and the other player is declared the winner.

Spam Musubi

PREP AND COOKING TIME: 1 HOUR 15 MIN · SOAK TIME: 4 HOURS
MAKES 10 PIECES

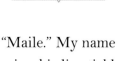

2 cups uncooked short-grain white rice

2 cups water

¾ cup white vinegar

½ cup granulated sugar

¼ cup soy sauce

¼ cup oyster sauce or fish sauce

1 (12-ounce) container Spam

2 tablespoons olive oil

5 sheets dry seaweed (sushi nori)

1. In a medium-size bowl, add rice and enough water to completely cover rice. Soak for 4 hours. Drain and rinse.

2. In a medium pan, bring 2 cups water to a boil. Add rice and stir. Reduce heat to medium-low, cover and simmer for 20 minutes.

3. Remove pan from heat and stir in white vinegar. Set aside and allow rice to cool completely.

4. In a medium bowl, whisk together sugar, soy sauce, and oyster sauce until sugar is completely dissolved.

5. Slice Spam into 10 slices, ¼-inch thick.

6. Heat oil in a large skillet over medium heat. Add sauce to slices and then cook 3 minutes per side or until light brown.

7. Cut noir sheets in half and lay flat. Form a rice patty roughly the same size as the meat slices. Place rice patty on noir sheet. Add a meat slice. Wrap noir around the rice and meat, sealing the edges with a touch of water. Serve warm or chilled.

VARIATIONS

- Instead of soy sauce marinade, use ¼ cup barbecue sauce or Huli-Huli sauce.
- For an additional crunch, shake on furikake (a Japanese seasoning blend made from sesame seeds, seaweed, herbs, fish flakes, dried mushrooms, salt, and sugar) before serving.

DID YOU KNOW? August 8th is considered National Spam Musubi day.

NOTE

- For faster preparation, purchase pre-made sticky rice and cook according to package direction.

"Maile." My name leaving his lips tickles my skin. It sounds like the resonating echo of a lover's flute, calling to me.

A SONG FOR THE STARS
Ilima Todd

Coconut Cake with Chocolate Ganache

PREP AND COOKING TIME: 2 HOURS · FREEZE TIME: OVERNIGHT
SERVES 16

CAKE

4 large eggs, separated

1 cup butter, softened

1¾ cups granulated sugar

1 cup cream of coconut, divided

2½ cups all-purpose flour

½ teaspoon salt

1 teaspoon baking powder

½ teaspoon baking soda

1 cup buttermilk

1 teaspoon coconut extract

COCONUT CREAM-CHEESE FROSTING

8 ounces cream cheese, softened

½ cup butter, softened

1 teaspoon coconut extract

1 (32-ounce) package powdered sugar

2 to 3 tablespoons milk

CHOCOLATE GANACHE

1 cup heavy whipping cream

8 ounces semisweet chocolate chips

TOASTED COCONUT

7 ounces sweetened, shredded coconut

1. **For the cake:** Separate eggs and set aside egg whites.
2. In a large mixing bowl, beat together egg yolks, butter, granulated sugar and ½ cup cream of coconut until fluffy. Set aside.
3. In a separate bowl, sift together flour, salt, baking powder, and baking soda. Stir well. Set aside.
4. In a small bowl, combine buttermilk and coconut extract. Set aside.
5. Using a stand mixer, alternate adding the dry ingredients and the buttermilk mixture to the egg mixture on low speed.
6. In a separate bowl, beat the egg whites with a pinch of salt until stiff. Gently fold egg whites into cake batter.
7. Spray two 9-inch round baking pans with a nonstick baking spray with flour. Pour batter into pans.
8. Bake at 275 degrees F. for 60 minutes. If cake tester or toothpick inserted in the center of the cake comes out clean, remove from oven. If not, continue to bake in additional 5-minute intervals until tester comes out clean.

CONTINUED ON PAGE 173

He kisses me again. And again. Each time is a little different. Each time a new form of surprise and pleasure mingles into a head-spinning bliss.

A SONG FOR THE STARS
Ilima Todd

9. Poke holes into each cake with the cake tester or a skewer, making sure not to go all the way through the cake. Drizzle remaining cream of coconut over the top.

10. Transfer cakes from pan to a wire rack and allow to cool completely. Then gently wrap cakes with both plastic wrap and aluminum foil and freeze overnight.

11. **For the frosting:** Using a stand mixer, beat the cream cheese, butter, and coconut extract. Add powdered sugar by the cupful until consistency is smooth. If the frosting becomes too stiff, add a tablespoon of milk. Set aside.

12. **For the ganache:** In a small saucepan over medium heat, bring heavy whipping cream just to a simmer, stirring occasionally. As soon as whipping cream begins to simmer, remove from heat and add chocolate chips. Cover saucepan and allow to sit 5 minutes. Do not mix. Uncover and whisk whipping cream and chocolate together until smooth. Allow ganache to sit 15 minutes at room temperature.

13. **To toast the coconut:** Spread coconut evenly in a single layer on a cookie sheet lined with parchment paper. Bake at 325 degrees F. for 8 to 10 minutes, or until some of the coconut turns slightly brown. Do not burn.

14. **To assemble the cake:** Remove cake from freezer. Place one layer on a serving platter.

15. Place 1 cup of frosting in the center of the cake and frost to the edges. Add the second layer of cake. Use the rest of the frosting to cover the cake.

16. Pour cooled ganache over the top of the frosted cake.

17. Sprinkle toasted coconut on top of the ganache.

18. Allow cake to thaw for at least an hour to bring the cake to room temperature before serving.

Fall Harvest

Caramel Apple Cider

PREP AND COOKING TIME: 5 MIN · SERVES 4 TO 6

CIDER

1 cup heavy whipping cream

2 tablespoons brown sugar

3 cups apple juice or apple cider

½ cup water

BROWN-SUGAR WHIPPED CREAM

¾ cup heavy whipping cream

¼ cup brown sugar

1 teaspoon vanilla extract

pinch of salt

1. **For the cider:** In a medium-size saucepan over medium-high heat, add whipping cream and brown sugar. Bring to a boil.

2. Add apple juice or cider and water and stir. Heat until mixture begins to steam. Remove from heat.

3. **For the whipped cream:** In a stand mixer or using a hand mixer with a bowl, combine whipping cream, brown sugar, vanilla, and salt. Whip on medium-high speed for 5 minutes or until thick and fluffy.

4. Pour cider into individual mugs and top with whipped cream.

DID YOU KNOW? Bobbing for apples was once a courting ritual. Each person would mark an apple, and then the person bobbing would try to bite the apple of their lover. If they could bite the apple on the first try, it meant the couple was made for each other.

Her stomach erupted in butterflies again, and it was all she could do to keep her hand from shaking as she lifted her glass and took a drink in an attempt to cover her reaction. She tried not to look at him for the rest of the dinner, but between courses and conversations she kept finding her gaze drifting toward him again and again.

LORD FENTON'S FOLLY
Josi S. Kilpack

Tomato Pesto Soup with Grilled-Cheese Croutons

PREP AND COOKING TIME: 1 HOUR 20 MIN · SERVES 8

SOUP

3 tablespoons olive oil

2 medium onions, chopped

3 (14-ounce) cans diced tomatoes

2 cups chicken stock

1 teaspoon dried parsley

½ cup whipping cream

1 cup basil pesto, prepared

salt and pepper to taste

GRILLED-CHEESE CROUTONS

1 tablespoon butter, softened

4 slices sourdough bread

4 ounces sharp cheddar cheese

1. **For the soup:** Heat oil in a large pan. Add chopped onion and cook on medium-low heat 8 to 12 minutes or until onion is translucent.

2. Add tomatoes and bring to a simmer.

3. Add chicken stock and parsley. Simmer 15 minutes. Stir in cream and pesto.

4. Pour soup into a blender or using an immersion blender, blend until smooth. Add salt and pepper to taste.

5. **For the croutons:** Spread the butter over one side of each slice of bread.

6. Heat a large frying pan over medium heat. Add two slices of bread, buttered-side down. Top with cheese and cover with the other two slices of bread, butter-side up.

7. Cook for 2 to 3 minutes, or until the bottom slice of bread is golden brown. Flip sandwiches over and cook another 2 to 3 minutes, until both sides are golden brown and the cheese is melted.

8. Remove grilled cheese sandwiches from the pan and allow to cool 5 minutes. Cut sandwiches into 1-inch croutons. Serve with soup.

VARIATIONS

- Instead of making grilled-cheese croutons, serve soup with slices of crusty bread and shaved Parmesan cheese. For extra crunch, add toasted pine nuts to the soup.
- For a holiday or special occasion, use cookie cutters to cut croutons into different shapes.
- Substitute cheddar cheese with Monterey Jack, Gouda, Havarti, or Swiss cheese.
- Substitute sourdough bread with whole wheat, rye, multigrain, or even gluten-free bread.

He'd intended to kiss her after whispering the endearment. But she kissed him first. She slid her hand into his hair, pressed her lips to his, and kissed him with every ounce of fervor he felt. There was nothing for it but to kiss her in return.

THE TIDES OF TIME
Sarah M. Eden

Glazed Carrots

PREP AND COOKING TIME: 20 MIN · SERVES 6

1½ pounds carrots, peeled and cut into ½-inch-thick slices

¼ cup butter

¼ cup brown sugar

¼ teaspoon salt

I leaned over the arm of my chair and looked into the most beautiful eyes I had ever seen.

HEIR TO EDENBROOKE
Julianne Donaldson

1. Add carrots to a large saucepan and cover with 1 to 2 inches of water.

2. Bring to a simmer and cook for 8 to 10 minutes or until carrots are tender. Drain.

3. Add butter, brown sugar, and salt to the pan. Stir until carrots are fully coated.

4. Cook an additional 5 to 6 minutes, on medium-low heat, stirring occasionally, until a sauce has formed.

5. Transfer carrots to a serving dish, pour sauce from pan over carrots, and serve.

VARIATIONS

- Instead of brown sugar, use ¼ cup honey or maple syrup.
- This recipe also works well with other root vegetables, such as parsnips and sweet potatoes.
- For a bit of crunch, sprinkle ¼ cup toasted and chopped pecans or almonds on top as well as a dash of cinnamon before serving.
- Sprinkle a tablespoon of chopped fresh parsley as garnish before serving.

> **DID YOU KNOW?** During the Victorian Era, pumpkins were not only carved as decorations but if one was delivered to your doorstep, it served as an invitation to a party.

NOTES

- Instead of slicing whole carrots, use bagged baby carrots. Make sure to cut carrots into uniformly sized pieces so they cook at the same rate.

Italian Meat Loaf

PREP AND COOKING TIME: 1 HOUR 30 MIN · SERVES 4 TO 6

MEAT LOAF

1½ pounds ground beef

½ cup Italian bread crumbs

½ cup shredded Parmesan cheese

1 (1-ounce) package dried onion soup

¼ cup sweet BBQ sauce

1 clove garlic, minced

1 egg

8 thin slices deli ham

8 thin slices provolone cheese

black pepper to taste

GLAZE

¼ cup ketchup

1 teaspoon brown mustard

1 tablespoon brown sugar

⅛ teaspoon liquid smoke or soy sauce (optional)

1. **For the meat loaf:** In a large bowl, mix ground beef, bread crumbs, Parmesan cheese, onion soup, BBQ sauce, garlic, egg, and black pepper.

2. On a cutting board or wax paper, flatten ground beef mixture into a square about ½-inch thick.

3. Layer ham and cheese slices over the ground beef mixture.

4. Roll the meat into a loaf, sealing the ends.

5. Place loaf a baking dish, seam-side down, and bake at 350 degrees F. for 45 minutes. Remove from oven.

6. **For the glaze:** In a small bowl, mix ketchup, brown mustard, and brown sugar. Add liquid smoke or soy sauce if desired.

7. Brush glaze over the top of the meat loaf.

8. Return meat loaf to the oven and cook an additional 15 minutes. Remove from oven and allow to cool in the pan for 10 minutes.

9. Slice and serve.

He was such a dark and handsome towering wall of man surrounded by mystery.

TO LOVE THE BROODING BARON
Jentry Flint

Halloween
Games

BLINDFOLDS
For 4+ players

One player is blindfolded and then spun in a circle by the other players. The blindfolded player then must make their way across the room to a table where several saucers have been placed, each one holding a different item. What the person selects determines what will happen before the next Halloween.

- A ring means they will marry soon.
- A lump of clay means they will die within the year.
- A cup of water means they will travel across the ocean.
- A string of rosary beads means they will join a religious order.
- A coin means they will become wealthy.
- A bean means they will endure poverty.

GHOST STORIES

Players gather around a fireplace. Each player selects a twig. The first player lights the tip of their twig and tells a ghost story for as long as the flame burns. Once it goes out, the next person lights their twig and continues the story until all the players have contributed to the story.

Pumpkin Cake with Cream Cheese Frosting

PREP AND COOKING TIME: 1 HOUR • SERVES 24

CAKE

2 cups all-purpose flour

1 teaspoon salt

1 teaspoon baking soda

1 teaspoon cinnamon

2 teaspoons baking powder

2 cups granulated sugar

1 cup vegetable or canola oil

4 large eggs

2 cups pumpkin puree

1 teaspoon vanilla extract

FROSTING

4 ounces cream cheese, softened

6 tablespoons butter, softened

3 cups powdered sugar

1 teaspoon vanilla extract

2 tablespoons milk

1. **For the cake:** In a mixing bowl, sift together flour, salt, baking soda, cinnamon, and baking powder. Set aside.

2. In a large mixing bowl or stand mixer, mix sugar and oil until combined. Add eggs, pumpkin puree, and vanilla and mix well.

3. Add flour mixture to the pumpkin mixture and mix until combined. Do not overmix.

4. Using a nonstick cooking spray with flour, coat a 15x10x1 baking sheet (jelly roll pan). Pour cake batter into prepared pan and bake at 350 degrees F. for 20 to 25 minutes. Cake will gently spring back in the center when done. Allow cake to cool completely.

5. **For the frosting:** In a medium mixing bowl, beat cream cheese until smooth. Add butter, powdered sugar, and vanilla. Combine. Add milk a little at a time until frosting is smooth.

6. Frost cake and serve.

VARIATIONS

• Add 1 cup chopped toasted nuts or 1 cup mini chocolate chips to either the cake batter or frosting.

This morning felt different. New. For the first time in a long time, I sat and simply watched rays of sunshine beaming through leaves on the trees. A warm, cozy spot, and several deep breaths rejuvenated me, and I felt so content to simply be.

HIGHCLIFFE HOUSE
Megan Walker

Pumpkin Trifle

ASSEMBLY TIME: 30 MIN · CHILL TIME: 1 HOUR · SERVES 12 TO 16

CAKE

1 recipe Pumpkin Cake
(see page 183)

SPICED PUMPKIN CREAM-CHEESE FILLING

8 ounces cream cheese, softened

½ cup pumpkin puree

¼ cup brown sugar

¾ teaspoon pumpkin pie spice

½ teaspoon vanilla extract

pinch of salt

WHIPPING CREAM

2 cups heavy whipping cream

⅓ cup powdered sugar

½ teaspoon vanilla extract

pinch of salt

8 ounces toffee candy bits

1. **For the cake:** Bake pumpkin cake as instructed. Do not frost. Once cooled, cut into 1-inch cubes.

2. **For the filling:** In a medium mixing bowl, beat the cream cheese, pumpkin puree, and brown sugar until smooth. Add pumpkin pie spice, vanilla, and salt.

3. Cover and refrigerate at least one hour.

4. **For the whipping cream:** Place whipping cream and powdered sugar in a chilled glass bowl and mix on high for 1 to 2 minutes. Add vanilla and salt and mix for an additional 1 to 2 minutes or until soft peaks have formed. Do not over-whip.

5. Refrigerate until you are ready to assemble the trifle.

6. **To assemble the trifle:** In a trifle bowl or glass serving bowl, layer cake cubes, ½ of the pumpkin cream-cheese filling, ½ of the whipping cream, and ½ of the toffee candy bits. Repeat.

> I didn't dare look up because I couldn't trust myself to not grab him by the collar and kiss him until he pulled away.
>
> ### LIES, LOVE, AND BREAKFAST AT TIFFANY'S
> *Julie Wright*

DID YOU KNOW? The early Americans in New England baked their pumpkin pies inside a hollowed-out pumpkin shell, though by 1796, the dessert had settled into the dish we know today.

NOTES

· Instead of using a large trifle bowl, serve this dessert in individual cups.

· Refrigerate assembled trifle until ready to serve.

Apple Pie Bar with Caramel Sauce

PREP AND COOKING TIME: 1 HOUR 25 MIN · SERVES 24

DOUGH

2¼ cups all-purpose flour

¾ teaspoon salt

⅔ cup butter-flavored shortening

8 tablespoons cold water

FILLING

10 cups chopped apples, peeled, cored, and cut into ¼-inch thick slices

⅔ cup granulated sugar

⅓ cup all-purpose flour

1 teaspoon ground cinnamon

1 cup rolled oats

CRUMB TOPPING

1 cup packed brown sugar

½ cup all-purpose flour

1 cup quick-cooking rolled oats

½ cup butter

CARAMEL SAUCE

4 tablespoons butter

1 cup brown sugar

½ cup half-and-half

1 tablespoon vanilla extract

pinch of salt

1. **For the dough:** In a large mixing bowl, combine flour and salt. Using a pastry blender, fork, or your hands, cut the shortening into the flour mixture until it resembles coarse crumbs. Sprinkle 1 tablespoon of cold water over the mixture and toss with a fork. Repeat using 1 tablespoon of water at a time until dough is moistened. Knead dough into a ball.

2. On a lightly floured surface, roll dough into a rectangle large enough to fill a jelly roll pan.

3. Spray a 15x10x1 pan with nonstick cooking spray. Wrap dough around rolling pin and unroll into the prepared pan. Spread dough over the pan and up the sides, being careful not to stretch or break it.

4. **For the filling:** In a large bowl, combine sliced apples, rolled oats, flour, and cinnamon. Stir until apples are coated.

5. Spoon the mixture over the prepared dough and spread evenly.

6. **For the crumb topping:** In a large bowl, combine the brown sugar, flour, and rolled oats. Using a fork or pastry blender, cut butter into oat mixture until topping resembles coarse crumbs. Sprinkle on top of apples.

Before she was finished saying his name, he brought his lips to hers. First, a feathery light touch, a memory of a dream. Then, when she lifted herself up on her toes to get closer to him, he wrapped his arms around her, kissing her fully and deeply.

WHISPERS OF SHADOWBROOK HOUSE
Rebecca Anderson

7. Bake at 375 degrees F. for 40 to 45 minutes, or until apples are tender. If the pie is starting to brown too fast, cover with aluminum foil for the last 5 to 10 minutes. Cool pie on wire rack.

8. **For the caramel sauce:** Gently whisk all ingredients in a medium saucepan over medium-low to medium-high heat for 5 to 8 minutes, until thick. Remove from heat and allow to cool slightly. Drizzle on top of pie and serve.

NOTES

· Both sweet and tart apples—or a mixture of both—work well in this recipe: Granny Smith, Gala, Honeycrisp, Jonagold, Braeburn, or Cortland.
· Instead of making a caramel sauce, a store-bought sauce will also work. Serve with vanilla ice cream or whipping cream.

DID YOU KNOW? Halloween has its roots in the ancient Celtic celebration of Samhain, which lasted from October 31 to November 1 and welcomed in the harvest.

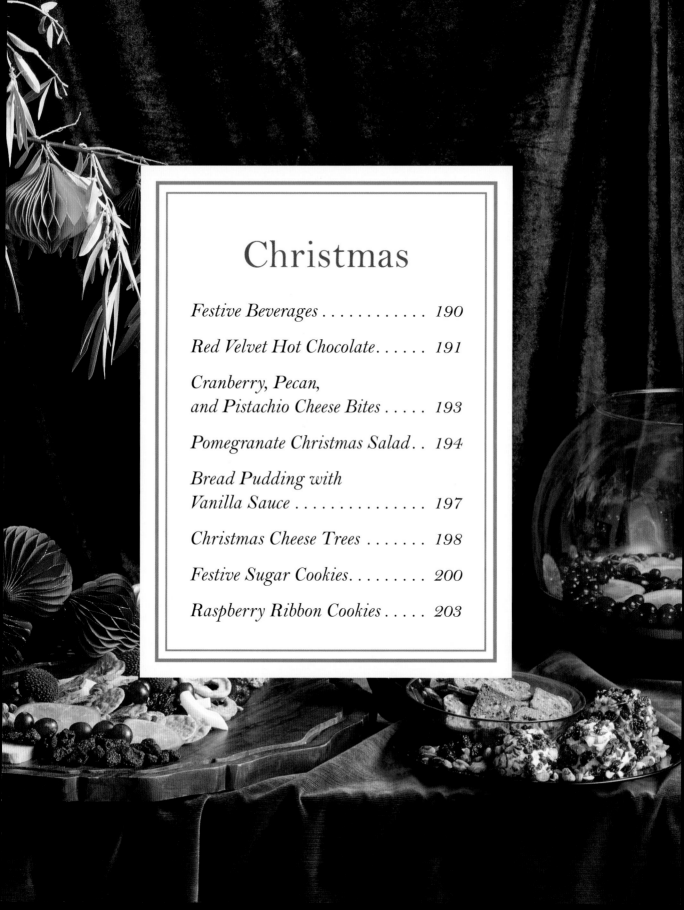

Christmas

Festive Beverages

HOLIDAY PUNCH

PREP TIME: 5 MIN · SERVES 12

6 cups cranberry juice or pomegranate-cranberry juice

3 cups pineapple juice

1 tablespoon almond extract

3 liters ginger ale

1 (12-ounce) bag fresh or frozen cranberries (optional)

2 fresh limes, thinly sliced (optional)

1. In a large pitcher or punch bowl, combine juices and almond extract. Add ginger ale and stir.

2. Add cranberries and limes.

3. Add ice as needed and serve within an hour.

LIMEADE SLUSH

PREP TIME: 10 MIN · CHILL TIME: 1 TO 2 HOURS · SERVES 40

3 cups granulated sugar

1 (12-ounce) can frozen limeade concentrate

8 cups hot water

4 liters lemon-lime soda

1. In a large pitcher, dissolve sugar and limeade in hot water. Pour into containers or ice-cube trays to freeze.

2. Add frozen cubes to punch bowl. Add lemon-lime soda and serve.

PARTY PUNCH

PREP TIME: 10 MIN · CHILL TIME: 2 TO 3 HOURS · SERVES 40

3 ripe bananas

3 cups warm water

2 cups granulated sugar

1½ cups orange juice

¼ cup lemon juice

1 (46-ounce) can pineapple juice

4 liters ginger ale

1. In blender, blend the bananas, water, and sugar until smooth. Pour into a large, freezer-safe container.

2. Add orange, lemon, and pineapple juices and mix well.

3. Freeze mixture, stirring every 30 minutes, until slushy.

4. Pour into a punch bowl and mix with ginger ale.

NOTES

· Freezing is optional.

· Punch can be frozen in a few small containers without stirring. Remove from freezer 1 to 2 hours before serving.

As they neared the refreshment table, Sophia noted a man lavishly attired as a maharaja, his clothing a blending of purple, orange, and blue silks.

THE SECRET OF THE INDIA ORCHID
Nancy Campbell Allen

Red Velvet Hot Chocolate

PREP AND COOKING TIME: 12 MIN · SERVES 4

HOT CHOCOLATE

2 cups milk

2 cups heavy whipping cream

1 cup chopped semisweet chocolate bar or chocolate chips

2 ounces white chocolate sauce

1 teaspoon red food coloring

1 teaspoon vanilla extract

MARSHMALLOW WHIPPING CREAM

1 cup heavy cream

6 ounces cream cheese, at room temperature

½ cup marshmallow crème

1 teaspoon vanilla extract

1. **For the hot chocolate:** In a small saucepan, bring milk and heavy whipping cream to a simmer. Add chocolate and chocolate sauce and cook on medium heat for about 10 minutes, stirring, until smooth. Add food coloring and vanilla and stir until combined. Whisk until frothy.

2. **For the whipping cream:** In a stand mixer or a hand mixer with a large bowl, whip together cream and cream cheese until soft peaks form. Fold in marshmallow crème and vanilla.

3. Pour hot chocolate into individual mugs and top with whipped cream.

VARIATION

• Instead of semisweet chocolate, use milk chocolate.

I reached up and touched his cheek with my fingers warm from the hot chocolate. "I like this face. This is a good face." . . . The kiss was warm and comfortable and delicious.

CHECK ME OUT
Becca Wilhite

DID YOU KNOW? The tradition of decorating Christmas trees is credited with originating in Germany in the sixteenth century, but it was popularized in England by Queen Victoria and Prince Albert after their marriage in 1840.

Cranberry, Pecan, and Pistachio Cheese Bites

PREP AND COOKING TIME: 20 MIN · CHILL TIME: 1 HOUR · SERVES 8

⅓ cup dried cranberries, chopped, divided

½ cup pecans, chopped, divided

½ cup pistachios, chopped, divided

8 ounces cream cheese, softened

1 cup white cheddar cheese

2 tablespoons chopped chives, or thinly sliced scallions, chopped (chop extra for the coating)

1. Chop dried cranberries, pecans, and pistachios. Reserve a couple of tablespoons of each in a small bowl and set aside.

2. In a food processor or a stand mixer with a large bowl, add cream cheese, cheddar cheese, cranberries, pecans, pistachios, and chives or scallions. Mix until well combined.

3. Wrap cheese mix in plastic and roll into balls. Refrigerate at least 1 hour, or until set.

4. Spread remaining mixture of cranberries, pecans, pistachios, and chives onto a clean surface. Remove plastic wrap from cheese and roll over chopped mixture until well covered.

5. Serve with crostini or a hearty cracker topped with cheese.

VARIATIONS

- Serve cheese with any fruit spread (cranberry, blueberry, or peach) or with a drizzle of honey.
- Can also be rolled into logs and sliced into wheels.

DID YOU KNOW? The traditional British "Christmas Crackers"—cardboard tubes wrapped in colorful paper and filled with paper hats, small sweets, and a silly joke— were invented by Tom Smith in 1845.

"Mistletoe is an invitation for kissing at Christmas," Duncan said.

Hazel . . . said nothing, though her cheeks were on fire as she remembered the one kiss they had shared.

LOVE AND LAVENDER
Josi S. Kilpack

Pomegranate Christmas Salad

PREP TIME: 15 MIN · SERVES 8

1½ cups heavy whipping cream

⅓ cup powdered sugar

pinch of salt

½ teaspoon vanilla extract

2 to 3 bananas, sliced

2 to 3 pomegranates, seeded (reserve some for garnish)

4 to 6 apples, peeled, cored, and chopped (Honeycrisp or SugarBee)

½–1 cup toasted pecans (optional)

1. In a stand mixer or a hand mixer with a large bowl, whip heavy whipping cream until stiff. Add powdered sugar and salt and mix well. Fold in vanilla.

2. In a separate bowl, add chopped apples and top with whipped cream. Fold in bananas and pomegranate seeds until well incorporated.

3. When ready to serve, top salad with reserved pomegranate seeds and toasted pecans if desired.

VARIATIONS

- Add coconut or mandarin oranges in step 2. All fruit amounts can be increased or decreased based on personal preference.

She had found him attractive while looking at him during dinner, but now, with the two of them so close, she could see the wave in his dark hair and the gold flecks in his hazel eyes set aglow by the low light from the wall sconce. He was more than handsome. Painfully handsome.

A CAPTAIN FOR CAROLINE GRAY
Julie Wright

NOTES

- Salad can be refrigerated in an airtight container prior to serving.
- If desired, leave the apples unpeeled.
- To toast pecans, spread them in a single layer on a microwave-safe plate. Microwave in 30-second intervals for 2 minutes or until fragrant.

Victorian Christmas Game

THE GAME OF PLUM PUDDING
Invented by Charles H. Bennett in 1857

The group is divided into two teams, headed by "Sir Loin" and "General Kettle." Each captain recruits players to their team and bestows upon them a military title paired with a food item (for example, "General Goose," "Private Potato," or "Colonel Corkscrew"). For gentleman, the title is conferred by tapping a walking stick on his shoulder; for a lady, it is a kiss placed upon her cheek.

HOW TO PLAY: General Kettle takes a small plate or wooden disc—called "the plum pudding"—and begins a story. When he mentions the word "plum pudding," he spins the disc on the table and calls out the name of another player who must then continue both the story and prevent the plate from falling.

FORFEITS: There are five forfeits that may occur that will end a player's turn: failing to keep the plum pudding spinning, failing to speak of yourself with your title, failing to continue the story, failing to mention "plum pudding," and failing to call an "enemy" by the correct name.

PENALTIES: When a player earns a forfeit, one of the following penalties is applied:
- "Basted"—you are pursued around the room and beaten with a handkerchief
- "Seasoned"—you must kiss every lady in the room and be slapped on the cheek in return
- "Scrubbed"—you must ask every lady to kiss you, but if she refuses, she scrubs your face with a handkerchief; once you have earned a kiss, you may rejoin the game
- "Sharpened"—two gentlemen must try to prevent you from kissing the lady you have selected

The game ends when one team has earned a set number of forfeits.

Anders and I went to the kitchen. . . . We stood close together while we worked. And when I turned to set the peeled potatoes in the pan, Anders took my hand and tugged me close to him.

His mouth met mine with warm tenderness, then traced over my lips, my cheeks, and my jawline before going back to my lips. I didn't mind because, as a wise woman named Lillian once told me, "What's the point of being together if you're not caught kissing in the kitchen?" or something like that anyway.

We took our time with this kiss that sealed the beginning of this new chapter in our story. We took our time because that was the gift of happily ever after.

Time.

GLASS SLIPPERS, EVER AFTER, AND ME
Julie Wright

Bread Pudding with Vanilla Sauce

PREP AND COOKING TIME: 2 HOURS 20 MIN
CHILL TIME: 2 HOURS (OR OVERNIGHT) · SERVES 12

1 (16-ounce) loaf French bread

CUSTARD

3¾ cups whole milk

1½ cups heavy cream

7 large eggs

1¼ cup granulated sugar

1 teaspoon vanilla extract

Zest of 1 orange (optional)

VANILLA SAUCE

1½ cups half-and-half

1½ cups milk

12 large egg yolks

9 tablespoons sugar

3 teaspoons vanilla extract

1. Cube bread into 1½-inch cubes. Spread cubed bread onto cooking sheet and place in a 250-degree F. oven for 30 minutes. If bread is still too moist, allow bread to dry for another 10 minutes. Repeat as needed.

2. **For the custard:** In a large bowl, combine milk, cream, eggs, sugar, vanilla, and orange zest. Whisk until eggs are fully incorporated.

3. Pour custard mixture into a 2-quart baking dish and then add the dried bread cubes. Gently stir until bread is completely coated.

4. Cover the baking dish with foil and refrigerate at least 2 hours until the extra custard mixture has been soaked up by the bread.

5. Place covered baking dish in a large roasting pan. Fill roasting pan with water until it comes halfway up the sides of the baking dish. (This water bath prevents the custard from curdling.)

6. Bake at 350 degrees F. for 90 minutes, covered, or until a toothpick inserted in the middle comes out clean.

7. Uncover baking dish and continue baking in the roasting pan for 10 minutes or until the crust becomes brown and crispy.

8. **For the sauce:** In a saucepan, add half-and-half and milk and bring to a simmer. Remove from heat.

9. In a medium bowl, whisk egg yolks and sugar together. Slowly stir in the warm milk mixture while whisking quickly. (Adding the milk too quickly will cook the egg yolks and cause the sauce to curdle.)

10. Return the mixture to the saucepan and cook over medium-low heat for 5 to 8 minutes, or until the sauce thickens and coats the back of a spoon.

11. Remove from heat. Stir in vanilla.

12. Top custard with warm vanilla sauce and serve.

I kissed her slowly, savoring the silky smoothness of her lips. I kissed her deeply, indulging in her intoxicating taste. . . . I couldn't hold her close enough, couldn't kiss her deeply enough. No, that would take me an entire lifetime.

The Making of an Earl, SUMMERHAVEN Collector's Edition
Tiffany Odekirk

Christmas Cheese Trees

PREP TIME: 10 MIN · SERVES 8

½ cup fresh herbs, finely chopped
(rosemary, basil, thyme)

1 teaspoon crushed red pepper
flakes

8 pretzel sticks

8 Brie wedges, white cheeses
(like provolone, Swiss, mozzarella),
or other soft cheese wedges

1. Blend chopped herbs and red pepper flakes on a shallow plate.

2. Secure pretzel stick at base of cheese wedge and press each side into the blend.

3. Serve immediately on a platter or charcuterie board.

DID YOU KNOW? King Edward VII
popularized the tradition of eating
turkey at Christmastime.

Fanny looked at
the wax-sealed wedge
of cheese and then lifted
her confused gaze
to meet the laughing
eyes of her cousin.
. . . "Mr. Longfellow
gave you a cheese?"

Jewett shook his head and
waved toward the parcel.
"He gave *you* a cheese."

FOREVER AND FOREVER
Josi S. Kilpack

Festive Sugar Cookies

PREP AND COOKING TIME: 1 HOUR 30 MIN
MAKES 3 TO 4 DOZEN COOKIES

COOKIES

4½ cups all-purpose flour	1 cup butter, softened
4 teaspoons baking powder	2 cups granulated sugar
½ teaspoon salt	2 large eggs
½ teaspoon baking soda	1 cup sour cream
¼ teaspoon ground nutmeg	1 teaspoon vanilla extract

FROSTING

2 cups butter, softened	6 cups powdered sugar
4 teaspoons vanilla extract	Food coloring (optional)
½ teaspoon salt	

1. **For the cookies:** In a large mixing bowl, sift together flour, baking powder, salt, baking soda, and ground nutmeg. Set aside.

2. In a stand mixer, cream together butter, sugar, and eggs. Add sour cream and vanilla. Mix well.

3. Add flour mixture to the butter mixture. Mix until combined.

4. With a floured rolling pin, roll out dough on a floured surface to ⅜- to ½-inch thick. Cut into desired shapes. Lift cookie dough with a spatula and transfer to a cookie sheet lined with parchment paper.

5. Bake at 350 degrees F. for 10 to 15 minutes, depending on thickness of the cookies. (It is normal for cookies to spread a little during baking.)

6. Transfer cookies to a wire rack and allow to cool completely.

7. **For the frosting:** In a large mixing bowl, add softened butter, vanilla, and salt. Cream together on medium speed for 30 seconds, or until blended.

8. Reduce mixer speed to low and add powdered sugar, 1 cup at a time, until fully incorporated.

9. Increase mixer speed to high and mix for 2 to 3 minutes until light and fluffy.

10. Add food coloring, if desired. (If you want more than one color, divide into different bowls.)

11. Frost cooled sugar cookies with a knife, or place frosting in a large piping bag with a metal tip and decorate.

Untouched pillows of snow topped shrubs and trees, and as they rounded a bend in the trail, more snow hugged the roof of the old, covered bridge, the railings, and the open window ledges, just as she had hoped.

MIRACLE CREEK CHRISTMAS
Krista Jensen

NOTE
· This recipe makes 4 cups of frosting, which should be enough to frost 4 dozen 2½-inch cookies.

VARIATION
· Add a few drops of almond, mint, lemon, or coconut extracts to the frosting for added flavor.
· Top frosted cookies with sprinkles or sanding sugar.

DID YOU KNOW? Christmas trees used to be decorated with apples, cookies, and other food. The disappearance of those treats gave rise to the idea that Santa had enjoyed a late-night snack while delivering presents. That custom evolved into the tradition of leaving out "milk and cookies" for Santa.

Raspberry Ribbon Cookies

PREP AND COOKING TIME: 45 MIN
CHILL TIME: 1 HOUR OR OVERNIGHT · MAKES 5 DOZEN COOKIES

COOKIES

1 cup butter, softened

½ cup granulated sugar

1 large egg

2 tablespoons milk

2 tablespoons vanilla extract

¼ teaspoon almond extract

2⅔ cups all-purpose flour, divided

6 tablespoons seedless raspberry jam or any other seedless jam

GLAZE

½ cup powdered sugar

1 tablespoon milk

1 teaspoon vanilla extract

1. **For the cookies:** In a stand mixer or a large mixing bowl, cream together butter and sugar on medium speed until light and fluffy. Add in egg, milk, and vanilla and almond extracts. Mix well.

2. Gradually add in 1½ cups flour. Beat at low speed until blended. Add enough remaining flour to form a stiff dough. Form dough into a disc and wrap in plastic. Refrigerate until firm, at least 1 hour or overnight.

3. Cut dough into 6 equal pieces. Rewrap 3 dough pieces and return to the refrigerator. With floured hands, shape each piece of dough into a 12-inch-long, ¾-inch-thick rope.

4. Place ropes 2 inches apart on an ungreased cookie sheet. Make a lengthwise ¼-inch-deep groove down the center of each rope with a finger or a wooden spoon handle. (Dough ropes will flatten to ½-inch-thick stripes.)

5. Bake at 375 degrees F. for 12 minutes. Remove from oven and spoon 1 tablespoon of jam into each groove.

6. Return to oven and bake an additional 5 to 7 minutes or until strips are a light golden-brown. Cool dough strips 15 minutes on cookie sheet.

7. **For the glaze:** In a small bowl, whisk powdered sugar, milk, and vanilla together until smooth.

8. Drizzle glaze over cooled cookie strips. Allow glaze to dry 5 to 10 minutes.

9. Cut cookie strips into 1-inch slices at a 45-degree angle. Transfer cookies to a wire rack and allow to cool completely.

10. Repeat with remaining dough.

11. Store tightly covered at room temperature between sheets of waxed paper or parchment paper.

She had told her cousins all about her day trip to Wickelston with the detective, and they had squealed with delight as they all sat in the middle of her bed and ate leftover dessert.

THE MATCHMAKER'S LONELY HEART
Nancy Campbell Allen

CELEBRATIONS: Christmas

ACKNOWLEDGMENTS

This cookbook would not have been possible without the incredible support and talent of so many people who helped bring it to life. Heidi Gordon, thank you for encouraging me to embark on this cookbook journey, finding the perfect concept, and always being there as a sounding board for my ideas. Heather Ward, your stunning design work has made this book truly special, from the beautiful cover to the thoughtfully crafted interior.

To Lisa Mangum and Bre Anderl, your editing, typesetting, and insightful contributions were invaluable. Alex Bingham, your creative vision in styling the cookbook and designing the amazing photo shoot backdrops brought this project to the next level, and Shane Huntsman, your photography skills captured the essence of this cookbook perfectly, delivering the best shots that made every page shine. Easton Madsen, thank you for your meticulous editing and invaluable assistance throughout the process. Laura Huff, your hard work during the photo shoot, along with your cherished friendship, has meant so much to me.

A special thanks to Erica Wright for always listening to my recipe ideas, offering feedback, and contributing to the creative process. To all my friends and family, past and present—your influence and support have been invaluable.

And finally, to my grandma, who first welcomed me into her kitchen all those years ago and sparked my love of baking—this book is for you.

INDEX

References to photographs and illustrations are in boldface.

INDEX

PROPER ROMANCE TITLES

REGENCY

Across the Star-Kissed Sea, Arlem Hawks
Blackmoore, Julianne Donaldson
Blackmoore, Collector's Edition,
    Julianne Donaldson
A Captain for Caroline Gray, Julie Wright
Edenbrooke, Julianne Donaldson
Edenbrooke, Collector's Edition,
    Julianne Donaldson
Games in a Ballroom, Jentry Flint
Georgana's Secret, Arlem Hawks
A Heart Revealed, Josi S. Kilpack
A Heart Worth Stealing, Joanna Barker
Heir to Edenbrooke, Julianne Donaldson
    (eBook)
Highcliffe House, Megan Walker
An Inconvenient Letter, Julie Wright
Lady Anna's Favor, Karen Tuft
A Lady's Favor, Josi S. Kilpack (eBook)
Lakeshire Park, Megan Walker
Lord Fenton's Folly, Josi S. Kilpack
*Matchmaking Mamas 3: The Gentleman's
    Confession*, Anneka R. Walker
*Matchmaking Mamas 4: The Rules of
    Matrimony*, Anneka R. Walker

Mayfield Family 1: Promises and Primroses,
    Josi S. Kilpack
Mayfield Family 2: Daisies and Devotion,
    Josi S. Kilpack
Mayfield Family 3: Rakes and Roses,
    Josi S. Kilpack
Mayfield Family 4: Love and Lavender,
    Josi S. Kilpack
Miss Newbury's List, Megan Walker
Miss Wilton's Waltz, Josi S. Kilpack
My Fair Gentleman,
    Nancy Campbell Allen
Promised, Leah Garriott
The Secret of the India Orchid,
    Nancy Campbell Allen
So True a Love, Joanna Barker
Summerhaven, Collector's Edition,
    Tiffany Odekirk
To Love the Brooding Baron, Jentry Flint
The Valet's Secret, Josi S. Kilpack
The Vicar's Daughter, Josi S. Kilpack
Windsong Manor, Julie Wright
Winterset, Tiffany Odekirk

VICTORIAN

The Art of Love and Lies, Rebecca Anderson

Ashes on the Moor, Sarah M. Eden

Ashes on the Moor, Collector's Edition,
   Sarah M. Eden

*The Dread Penny Society 1: The Lady and
   the Highwayman*, Sarah M. Eden

*The Dread Penny Society 2: The Gentleman
   and the Thief*, Sarah M. Eden

*The Dread Penny Society 3: The Merchant
   and the Rogue*, Sarah M. Eden

*The Dread Penny Society 4: The Bachelor
   and the Bride*, Sarah M. Eden

*The Dread Penny Society 5: The Queen
   and the Knave*, Sarah M. Eden

*The Dread Penny Society: The Complete
   Penny Dreadful Collection*,
   Sarah M. Eden

Isabelle and Alexander, Rebecca Anderson

The Matchmaker's Lonely Heart,
   Nancy Campbell Allen

The Orchids of Ashthorne Hall,
   Rebecca Anderson

Protecting Her Heart,
   Nancy Campbell Allen

The Tides of Time: A Storm Tide Romance,
   Sarah M. Eden

Whispers of Shadowbrook House,
   Rebecca Anderson

STEAMPUNK

Beauty and the Clockwork Beast,
   Nancy Campbell Allen

Brass Carriages and Glass Hearts,
   Nancy Campbell Allen

Kiss of the Spindle, Nancy Campbell Allen

The Lady in the Coppergate Tower,
   Nancy Campbell Allen

WESTERN

Healing Hearts, Sarah M. Eden

Longing for Home, Sarah M. Eden

Longing for Home 2: Hope Springs,
   Sarah M. Eden

The Sheriffs of Savage Wells, Sarah M. Eden

Wyoming Wild, Sarah M. Eden

CONTEMPORARY

Check Me Out, Becca Wilhite

Glass Slippers, Ever After, and Me,
   Julie Wright

Lies Jane Austen Told Me, Julie Wright

Lies, Love, and Breakfast at Tiffany's,
   Julie Wright

Miracle Creek Christmas, Krista Jensen

EDWARDIAN

Hearts of Briarwall, Krista Jensen

GEORGIAN

The Time Traveler's Masquerade,
   Sian Ann Bessey

HISTORICAL

All That Makes Life Bright, Josi S. Kilpack

Forever and Forever, Josi S. Kilpack

The Lady of the Lakes, Josi S. Kilpack

A Song for the Stars, Ilima Todd

ABOUT THE AUTHOR

MICHELLE WRIGHT grew up baking at her grandmother's side in a small Idaho kitchen and discovered early in life that there's no better way to combine creativity, love, and service than by mixing up some flour, sugar, butter, and chocolate—and then sharing those freshly baked cookies with neighbors and friends. Over the years, besides perfecting the chocolate chip cookie, she has expanded her repertoire to include more challenging recipes and feature more unique ingredients, such as infused olive oils and balsamic vinegars. But at her core, she still uses baking as a creative expression and an act of love. When she's not baking, she loves to travel the world, though that may secretly be another way to extend her love of good food, because her destinations and itineraries are always planned around trying the best local cuisine and finding a new regional cookbook to add to her collection. Her most cherished cookbook of all is the one she still uses from her grandmother's kitchen.